GED**X**celerator PREP

Writing

STUDENT BOOK

PAXEN

PAXEN

Melbourne, Florida
www.paxen.com

Acknowledgements

For each of the selections and images listed below, grateful acknowledgement is made for permission to excerpt and/or reprint original or copyrighted material, as follows:

Images

(cover, meeting preparation background) iStockphoto. **(cover, downtown scene)** Bilderbuch, DesignPics.com. **(cover, man typing)** Darren Greenwood, DesignPics.com. **v** iStockphoto. **vi** iStockphoto. **BLIND** Lynn Goldsmith/Corbis. **20** Getty Images. **38** Frazer Harrison/Getty Images. **66** Frank Trapper/Corbis. **94** Photo of Walter Anderson courtesy of PARADE.

ISBN-13: 978-1-934350-23-2
ISBN-10: 1-934350-23-0

2 3 4 5 6 7 8 9 10 GEDXSE5 16 15 14 13 12 11 10   Printed in the U.S.A.

Table of Contents

About the GED Tests

Simply by turning to this page, you've made a decision that will change your life for the better. Each year, thousands of people just like you decide to pursue the General Education Development (GED) certificate. Like you, they left school for one reason or another. And now, just like them, you've decided to continue your education by studying for and taking the GED Tests.

However, the GED Tests are no easy task. The tests—five in all, spread across the subject areas of Language Arts/Reading, Language Arts/Writing, Mathematics, Science, and Social Studies—cover slightly more than seven hours. Preparation time takes considerably longer. The payoff, however, is significant: more and better career options, higher earnings, and the sense of achievement that comes with a GED certificate. Employers and colleges and universities accept the GED certificate as they would a high school diploma. On average, GED recipients earn more than $4,000 per year than do employees without a GED certificate.

The GED Tests have been constructed by the American Council on Education (ACE) to mirror a high-school curriculum. Although you will not need to know all of the information typically taught in high school, you will need to answer a variety of questions in specific subject areas. In Language Arts/Writing, you will need to write an essay on a topic of general knowledge.

In all cases, you will need to effectively read and follow directions, correctly interpret questions, and critically examine answer options. The table below details the five subject areas, the amount of questions within each of them, and the time that you will have to answer them. Since different states have different requirements for the amount of tests you may take in a single day, you will need to check with your local adult education center for requirements in your state or territory.

The original GED Tests were released in 1942 and since have been revised a total of three times. In each case, revisions to the tests have occurred as a result of educational findings or workplace needs. All told, more than 17 million people have received a GED certificate since the tests' inception.

SUBJECT AREA BREAKDOWN	CONTENT AREAS	ITEMS	TIME LIMIT
Language Arts/Reading	Literary texts—75% Nonfiction texts—25%	40 questions	65 minutes
Language Arts/Writing (Editing)	Organization—15% Sentence Structure—30% Usage—30% Mechanics—25%	50 questions	75 minutes
Language Arts/Writing (Essay)	Essay	Essay	45 minutes
Mathematics	Number Sense/Operations—20% to 30% Data Measurement/Analysis—20% to 30% Algebra—20% to 30% Geometry—20% to 30%	Part I: 25 questions (with calculator) Part II: 25 questions (without calculator)	90 minutes
Science	Life Science—45% Earth/Space Science—20% Physical Science—35%	50 questions	80 minutes
Social Studies	Geography—15% U.S. History—25% World History—15% U.S. Government/Civics—25% Economics—20%	50 questions	70 minutes

Three of the subject-area tests—Language Arts/Reading, Science, and Social Studies—will require you to answer questions by interpreting passages. The Science and Social Studies Tests also require you to interpret tables, charts, graphs, diagrams, timelines, political cartoons, and other visuals. In Language Arts/Reading, you also will need to answer questions based on workplace and consumer texts. The Mathematics Test will require you to use basic computation, analysis, and reasoning skills to solve a variety of word problems, many of them involving graphics. On all of the tests, questions will be multiple-choice with five answer options. An example follows.

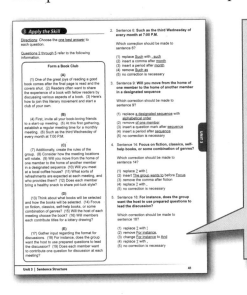

Sentence 18: **For instance, does the group want the host to use prepared questions to lead the discussion?**

Which correction should be made to sentence 18?

(1) replace ? with !
(2) remove For instance,
(3) change For instance to And
(4) replace ? with .
(5) no correction is necessary

On the Mathematics Test, you will have additional ways in which to register your responses to multiple-choice questions.

As the table on p. iv indicates, the Language Arts/ Writing Test contains two parts, one for editing, the other for essay. In the editing portion of Language Arts/ Writing, you will be asked to identify and correct common errors in various passages and texts while also deciding on the most effective organization of a text. In the essay portion, you will write an essay that provides an explanation or an opinion on a single topic of general knowledge.

Now that you understand the task at hand—and the benefits of a GED certificate—you must prepare for the GED Tests. In the pages that follow, you will find a recipe of sorts that, if followed, will help guide you toward successful completion of your GED certificate. So turn the page. The next chapter of your life begins right now.

About *GED Prep Xcelerator*

Along with choosing to pursue your GED certificate, you've made another smart decision by selecting *GED Prep Xcelerator* as your main study and preparation tool. Simply by purchasing *GED Prep Xcelerator*, you've joined an elite club with thousands of members, all with a common goal—earning their GED certificates. In this case, membership most definitely has its privileges.

For more than 65 years, the GED Tests have offered a second chance to people who need it most. To date, 17 million Americans like you have studied for and earned GED certificates and, in so doing, jump-started their lives and careers. Benefits abound for GED holders: Recent studies have shown that people with GED certificates earn more money, enjoy better health, and exhibit greater interest in and understanding of the world around them than those without.

In addition, more than 60 percent of GED recipients plan to further their educations, which will provide them with more and better career options. As if to underscore the point, U.S. Department of Labor projections show that 90 percent of the fastest-growing jobs through 2014 will require postsecondary education.

Your pathway to the future—a brighter future—begins now, on this page, with *GED Prep Xcelerator*, an intense, accelerated approach to GED preparation. Unlike other programs, which take months to teach the GED Tests through a content-based approach, *Xcelerator* gets to the heart of the GED Tests—and quickly—by emphasizing *concepts*. That's because at their core, the majority of the GED Tests are reading-comprehension exams. You must be able to read and interpret excerpts, passages, and various visuals—tables, charts, graphs, timelines, and so on—and then answer questions based upon them.

Xcelerator shows you the way. By emphasizing key reading and thinking concepts, *Xcelerator* equips learners like you with the skills and strategies you will need to correctly interpret and answer questions on the GED Tests. Two-page micro-lessons in each student book provide focused and efficient instruction, while call-out boxes, sample exercises, and test-taking and other thinking strategies aid in understanding complex concepts. For those who require additional support, we offer the *Xcelerator* workbooks, which provide twice the support and practice exercises as the student books.

Unlike other GED materials, which were designed for the classroom, *Xcelerator* materials were designed *from* the classroom, using proven educational theory and cutting-edge classroom philosophy. The result: More than 90 percent of people who study with *Xcelerator* earn their GED certificates. For learners who have long had the deck stacked against them, the odds are finally in their favor. And yours.

GED BY THE NUMBERS

17 million
Number of GED recipients since the inception of GED Tests

1.23 million
Amount of students who fail to graduate from high school each year

700,000
Number of GED test-takers each year

451,759
Total number of students who passed the GED Tests in 2007

$4,000
Average additional earnings per year for GED recipients

About *GED Prep Xcelerator Writing*

For those who think the GED Language Arts/Writing Test is a breeze, think again. The GED Language Arts/Writing Test is a multi-faceted exam that will assess your ability to both write and understand the basics of written text. The GED Language Arts/Writing Test consists of both an essay and an editing portion. You will have 45 minutes in which to complete an **essay,** or a short, personal piece of writing on a single subject. On the editing portion of the test, you will have 75 minutes in which to answer 50 multiple choice questions organized across four main content areas: Organization (15% of all questions), Sentence Structure (30%), Usage (30%), and (Mechanics (25%).

GED Prep Xcelerator Writing helps unlock the learning and deconstruct the different elements of the test by helping students like you to build and develop key reading and thinking skills. A combination of targeted strategies, informational call-outs and sample questions, assorted tips and hints (Test-Taking Tips and Writing Strategies), and ample assessment help to clearly focus your efforts in needed areas, all with an eye toward the end goal: Success on the GED Tests.

① Essay:

On the essay portion of the GED Language Arts/Writing Test, you must read a prompt, or writing topic, that will specify the topic and type of essay you are to write. The prompts will be **expository** in nature, meaning you must explain and describe your feelings about a particular topic. When doing so, ensure that you define your key point; organize your essay with a clear beginning, middle, and end; develop strong details that expertly support your main ideas; and use correct spelling, grammar, and punctuation.

Although writing is a process, it is a timed activity on the GED Language Arts/Writing Test. For that reason, you must manage your time well across all aspects of the essay. You will have 45 minutes in which to plan, write, and edit your essay. Note that Lesson 6 of the essay portion of this book contains a scoring rubric you may use to score your practice essays. This circle graph will help you visualize the amount of time you will be provided and how to use that time wisely.

5 minutes to read and edit the essay

10 minutes to plan the essay

30 minutes to write the essay

You will write your essay on a topic, or prompt, provided on the GED Language Arts/Writing Test. Many prompts will ask for your opinion on a topic of general interest. In the following cases, use your personal observations, experiences, and knowledge to help guide your writing:

- important people you would like to meet
- an invention that has affected your life
- good advice you have been given
- the season of the year you like best

Other prompts will ask you to think about certain aspects of your life. In the following instances, do not over-complicate things; simply write about what you know:

- family
- friends
- school
- hobbies
- sports
- pets

② Editing:

On the editing portion of the GED Language Arts/Writing Test, you will be asked to read and answer questions about letters, memoranda, and essays. The questions will focus on the areas of organization, sentence structure, usage, and mechanics as they relate to grammar and writing. **Grammar** is the set of rules that determines the usage of language.

The text, strategies, and tips in the *GED Prep Xcelerator Writing Student Book* are designed to provide structured and efficient practice in writing and editing. As you complete a unit, note the grammar rules you have learned. If you require additional support, consult the corresponding lesson in the *GED Prep Xcelerator Writing Workbook*.

The **Learn the Skill** section defines and provides additional information about the skill to be studied.

Callouts provide strategies and information that you may use to understand and interpret various passages or graphics.

Test-Taking Tips offer broad or specific support for answering multiple-choice questions.

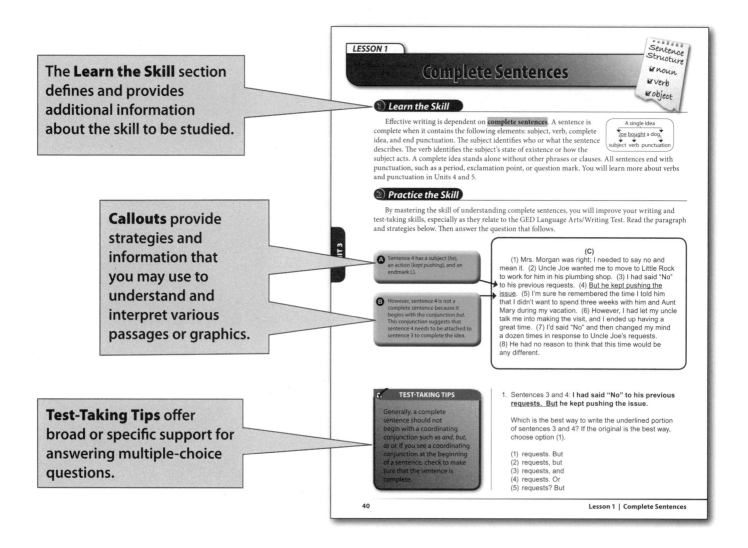

LESSON 1

Complete Sentences

Sentence Structure
☑ noun
☑ verb
☑ object

① Learn the Skill

Effective writing is dependent on **complete sentences**. A sentence is complete when it contains the following elements: subject, verb, complete idea, and end punctuation. The subject identifies who or what the sentence describes. The verb identifies the subject's state of existence or how the subject acts. A complete idea stands alone without other phrases or clauses. All sentences end with punctuation, such as a period, exclamation point, or question mark. You will learn more about verbs and punctuation in Units 4 and 5.

A single idea
Joe bought a dog.
subject verb punctuation

② Practice the Skill

By mastering the skill of understanding complete sentences, you will improve your writing and test-taking skills, especially as they relate to the GED Language Arts/Writing Test. Read the paragraph and strategies below. Then answer the question that follows.

A Sentence 4 has a subject (*he*), an action (*kept pushing*), and an endmark (*.*).

B However, sentence 4 is not a complete sentence because it begins with the conjunction *but*. This conjunction suggests that sentence 4 needs to be attached to sentence 3 to complete the idea.

(C)
(1) Mrs. Morgan was right; I needed to say no and mean it. (2) Uncle Joe wanted me to move to Little Rock to work for him in his plumbing shop. (3) I had said "No" to his previous requests. (4) But he kept pushing the issue. (5) I'm sure he remembered the time I told him that I didn't want to spend three weeks with him and Aunt Mary during my vacation. (6) However, I had let my uncle talk me into making the visit, and I ended up having a great time. (7) I'd said "No" and then changed my mind a dozen times in response to Uncle Joe's requests. (8) He had no reason to think that this time would be any different.

☑ **TEST-TAKING TIPS**

Generally, a complete sentence should not begin with a coordinating conjunction such as *and, but,* or *or.* If you see a coordinating conjunction at the beginning of a sentence, check to make sure that the sentence is complete.

1. Sentences 3 and 4: **I had said "No" to his previous requests. But he kept pushing the issue.**

   Which is the best way to write the underlined portion of sentences 3 and 4? If the original is the best way, choose option (1).

   (1) requests. But
   (2) requests, but
   (3) requests, and
   (4) requests. Or
   (5) requests? But

40   Lesson 1 | Complete Sentences

While it is important to learn grammar rules, it is also important to remember that English is an imperfect language, and there are exceptions to most rules. Remember to trust your instincts. Sometimes a sentence simply sounds wrong. If you forget a rule, read aloud the question and answers; if a sentence or series of words sounds incorrect, it probably is. Keep this in mind as you work through this book.

Each lesson in *GED Prep Xcelerator Writing* consists of questions that relate to the lesson's content. Most questions will provide you with a sentence from the paragraph, essay, letter, or memorandum on the same page. You then will be asked to find the best spelling, punctuation, or structure correction. You also may be asked to revise the placement of the sentence within the paragraph. Other questions will ask you to identify types or parts of sentences.

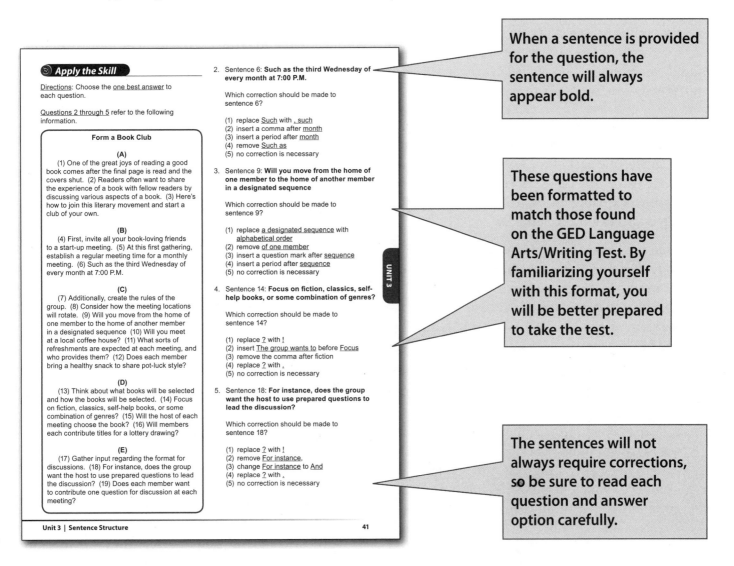

③ Apply the Skill

Directions: Choose the one best answer to each question.

Questions 2 through 5 refer to the following information.

Form a Book Club

(A)
(1) One of the great joys of reading a good book comes after the final page is read and the covers shut. (2) Readers often want to share the experience of a book with fellow readers by discussing various aspects of a book. (3) Here's how to join this literary movement and start a club of your own.

(B)
(4) First, invite all your book-loving friends to a start-up meeting. (5) At this first gathering, establish a regular meeting time for a monthly meeting. (6) Such as the third Wednesday of every month at 7:00 P.M.

(C)
(7) Additionally, create the rules of the group. (8) Consider how the meeting locations will rotate. (9) Will you move from the home of one member to the home of another member in a designated sequence (10) Will you meet at a local coffee house? (11) What sorts of refreshments are expected at each meeting, and who provides them? (12) Does each member bring a healthy snack to share pot-luck style?

(D)
(13) Think about what books will be selected and how the books will be selected. (14) Focus on fiction, classics, self-help books, or some combination of genres? (15) Will the host of each meeting choose the book? (16) Will members each contribute titles for a lottery drawing?

(E)
(17) Gather input regarding the format for discussions. (18) For instance, does the group want the host to use prepared questions to lead the discussion? (19) Does each member want to contribute one question for discussion at each meeting?

2. Sentence 6: **Such as the third Wednesday of every month at 7:00 P.M.**

   Which correction should be made to sentence 6?

   (1) replace Such with , such
   (2) insert a comma after month
   (3) insert a period after month
   (4) remove Such as
   (5) no correction is necessary

3. Sentence 9: **Will you move from the home of one member to the home of another member in a designated sequence**

   Which correction should be made to sentence 9?

   (1) replace a designated sequence with alphabetical order
   (2) remove of one member
   (3) insert a question mark after sequence
   (4) insert a period after sequence
   (5) no correction is necessary

4. Sentence 14: **Focus on fiction, classics, self-help books, or some combination of genres?**

   Which correction should be made to sentence 14?

   (1) replace ? with !
   (2) insert The group wants to before Focus
   (3) remove the comma after fiction
   (4) replace ? with .
   (5) no correction is necessary

5. Sentence 18: **For instance, does the group want the host to use prepared questions to lead the discussion?**

   Which correction should be made to sentence 18?

   (1) replace ? with !
   (2) remove For instance,
   (3) change For instance to And
   (4) replace ? with .
   (5) no correction is necessary

UNIT 3

Unit 3 | Sentence Structure   41

When a sentence is provided for the question, the sentence will always appear bold.

These questions have been formatted to match those found on the GED Language Arts/Writing Test. By familiarizing yourself with this format, you will be better prepared to take the test.

The sentences will not always require corrections, so be sure to read each question and answer option carefully.

Test-Taking Tips

The GED Tests include 240 questions across the five subject-area exams of Language Arts/Reading, Language Arts/Writing, Mathematics, Science, and Social Studies. In each of the GED Tests, you will need to apply some amount of subject-area knowledge. However, because all of the questions are multiple-choice items largely based on text or visuals (such as tables, charts, or graphs), the emphasis in *GED Prep Xcelerator* is on helping learners like you to build and develop core reading and thinking skills. As part of the overall strategy, various test-taking tips are included below and throughout the book to help you improve your performance on the GED Tests. For example:

◆ *Always thoroughly read the directions so that you know exactly what to do.* In Mathematics, for example, one part of the test allows for the use of a calculator. The other part does not. If you are unsure of what to do, ask the test provider if the directions can be explained.

◆ *Read each question carefully so that you fully understand what it is asking.* Some questions, for example, may present extra information that is unnecessary to correctly answer them. Other questions may note emphasis through capitalized and boldfaced words (Which of the following is **NOT** an example of photosynthesis?).

◆ *Manage your time with each question.* Because the GED Tests are timed exams, you'll want to spend enough time with each question, but not *too* much time. For example, on the GED Language Arts/Writing Test, you will have 75 minutes in which to answer 50 multiple-choice questions and 45 minutes to complete an essay. That works out to a little more than 90 seconds per question. You can save time by first reading each question and its answer options before reading the passage. Once you understand what the question is asking, review the passage for the appropriate information.

◆ *Answer all questions, regardless of whether you know the answer or are guessing at it.* There is no benefit in leaving questions unanswered on the GED Tests. Keep in mind the time that you have for each test and manage it accordingly. For time purposes, you may decide to initially skip questions. However, note them with a light mark beside the question and try to return to them before the end of the test.

◆ *Note any unfamiliar words in questions.* First attempt to re-read a question by omitting any unfamiliar word(s). Next, try to substitute another word in its place.

◆ *Narrow answer options by re-reading each question and the accompanying text or graphic.* Although all five answers are possible, keep in mind that only one of them is correct. You may be able to eliminate one or two answers immediately; others may take more time and involve the use of either logic or assumptions. In some cases, you may need to make your best guess between two options. If so, keep in mind that test-makers often avoid answer patterns; that is, if you know the previous answer is (2) and are unsure of the answer to the next question but have narrowed it to options (2) and (4), you may want to choose (4).

◆ *Read all answer choices.* Even though the first or second answer choice may appear to be correct, be sure to thoroughly read all five answer choices. Then go with your instinct when answering questions. For example, if your first instinct is to mark (1) in response to a question, it's best to stick with that answer unless you later determine that answer to be incorrect. Usually, the first answer you choose is the correct one.

◆ *Correctly complete your answer sheet by marking one numbered space on the answer sheet beside the number to which it corresponds.* Mark only one answer for each item; multiple answers will be scored as incorrect. If time permits, double-check your answer sheet after completing the test to ensure that you have made as many marks—no more, no less—as there are questions.

Study Skills

You've already made two very smart decisions in trying to earn your GED certificate and in purchasing *GED Prep Xcelerator* to help you do so. The following are additional strategies to help you optimize success on the GED Tests.

3 weeks out ...

- Set a study schedule for the GED Tests. Choose times in which you are most alert and places, such as a library, that provide the best study environment.

- Thoroughly review all material in *GED Prep Xcelerator*, using the *GED Prep Xcelerator Writing Workbook* to extend understanding of concepts in the *GED Prep Xcelerator Writing Student Book*.

- Make sure you have the necessary tools for the job: sharpened pencils, pens, paper, and, for Mathematics, the Casio-fx 260 Solar calculator.

- Keep notebooks for each of the subject areas you are studying. Folders with pockets are useful for storing loose papers.

- When taking notes, restate thoughts or ideas in your own words rather than copying them directly from a book. You can phrase these notes as complete sentences, as questions (with answers), or as fragments, provided you understand them.

- Take the pretests, noting any troublesome subject areas. Focus your remaining study around those subject areas.

1 week out ...

- Prepare the items you will need for the GED Tests: admission ticket (if necessary), acceptable form of identification, some sharpened No. 2 pencils (with erasers), a watch, eyeglasses (if necessary), a sweater or jacket, and a high-protein snack to eat during breaks.

- Map out the course to the test center, and visit it a day or two before your scheduled exam. If you drive, find a place to park at the center.

- Get a good night's sleep the night before the GED Tests. Studies have shown that learners with sufficient rest perform better in testing situations.

The day of ...

- Eat a hearty breakfast high in protein. As with the rest of your body, your brain needs ample energy to perform well.

- Arrive 30 minutes early to the testing center. This will allow sufficient time in the event of a change to a different testing classroom.

- Pack a sizeable lunch, especially if you plan to be at the testing center most of the day.

- Focus and relax. You've come this far, spending weeks preparing and studying for the GED Tests. It's your time to shine.

BILL COSBY

Earning his GED certificate paved the way for Cosby to excel in college, earning a Bachelor's, a Master's, and a Ph.D. degree.

Bill Cosby's sixth-grade teacher knew greatness when she saw it. As she would later recall of her former pupil, "William is a boy's boy, an all-around fellow, and he should grow up to do great things." Little did Cosby's teacher know how true her words would ring.

Cosby became a famous comedian, actor, author, and philanthropist—all despite leaving high school in 10th grade to join the U.S. Navy. Cosby earned his GED certificate while enlisted. After he was discharged from the Navy, he enrolled in Temple University, where he worked to become a physical education teacher. However, he had always been a talented comedian, and he left school to perform.

In the 1960s, Cosby made the leap from comedian to actor, and he changed the look of television. On the dramatic television series *I SPY*, Cosby played the first African American character to be the equal of a white character. He went on to do several more television programs, most notably *The Cosby Show*, a situation comedy about an affluent African American family. One of Cosby's goals with the program was to present the idea that,

> **"People are many things simultaneously. 'Race' is one such thing, but it isn't the only one and it isn't always the primary one."**

Cosby starred in several other television shows and movies and authored several books. He promotes education, personal responsibility, and parenting as a means to empower lower-income families in the United States.

BIO BLAST: Bill Cosby

- Born on July 12, 1937, in Philadelphia, Pennsylvania
- Left high school in 10th grade to join the U.S. Navy, where he earned his GED certificate
- Is well-known for his social activism

- Recorded many top-selling comedy albums
- Authored several best-selling books, including *Fatherhood*
- Created the Ennis William Cosby Foundation to assist students with language-learning differences

Unit 1: Essay

In order to write a strong essay on the GED Language Arts/Writing Test, it is important to understand all the components of an essay. A complete essay for the GED Test consists of five paragraphs. The first paragraph is the **introduction**. It provides the reader with a **thesis statement**, or main idea, and the three **supporting details** that help support the thesis statement. The second, third, and fourth paragraphs make up the **body**. The body of an essay provides the reader with the explanation and elaboration of each supporting detail. Each body paragraph is dedicated to one supporting detail. The final paragraph in the five-paragraph essay is the **conclusion**. The conclusion is the essay's summary. The thesis statement and three supporting details should be restated and the paragraph should end with something memorable: a quote, an anecdote, or an insightful thought. For a visual representation of an essay, see the graphic organizer on the right.

Essay Graphic Organizer

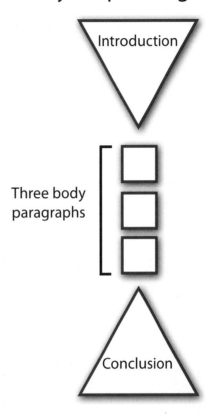

Introduction

Three body paragraphs

Conclusion

Table of Contents

Develop Thesis Statement

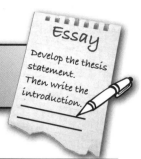

Essay
Develop the thesis statement. Then write the introduction.

① Learn

The **thesis statement** introduces the topic of your essay. The **supporting details** provide support to the thesis statement. You will learn more about supporting details in Unit 2. As a writer you can refer back to the thesis statement to keep you focused on the topic of the essay. Remember that while all paragraphs in your essay may have a main idea, the essay has only one thesis statement.

② Practice

By mastering these components, you will improve your writing and test-taking skills, especially as they relate to the GED Language Arts/Writing Test. Read the paragraph below. Then answer the question that follows.

A thesis statement makes a specific point about the topic and should be stated clearly and concisely. Although it typically appears in the beginning of the first paragraph, it can also appear in the middle.

Using a mental map, like the one below, will help you brainstorm ideas.

Thesis Statement:
Mean what you say

Supporting detail: *My dog, Scout*

Supporting detail: *My future*

Supporting detail: *My Uncle Joe*

 WRITING STRATEGIES

When trying to formulate a thesis statement, it is best to refer to the prompt. It will help you determine what to write about in your essay.

Prompt: Everyone has received advice from a parent, friend, teacher, or co-worker.

Identify one piece of advice that someone has shared with you. Explain when and why the advice was given, how you applied the advice, and whether the advice was valuable. To develop your essay, use your own observations, experiences, and knowledge.

(A)

(1) Many teenagers today do not heed the advice of their parents. (2) Instead, they are more likely to follow advice from a friend or an adult they trust. (3) Last year, I asked Mrs. Morgan, my former social studies teacher, advice on whether or not I should stay with my Uncle Joe and become a plumber. (4) Mrs. Morgan said to me, "Whatever you decide, just make sure you mean what you say." (5) This year, the best advice I have been given is to mean what I say. (6) It helped me make the right decision with my dog Scout, my Uncle Joe, and my future.

1. Which of the following sentences is the thesis statement?

   (1) Instead, they are more likely to follow advice from a friend or an adult they trust.
   (2) Last year, I asked Mrs. Morgan, my former social studies teacher, advice on whether or not I should stay with my Uncle Joe and become a plumber.
   (3) Mrs. Morgan said to me, "Whatever you decide, just make sure you mean what you say."
   (4) This year, the best advice I have been given is to mean what I say.
   (5) It helped me make the right decision with my dog Scout, my Uncle Joe, and my future.

Directions: On the GED Language Arts/Writing Test, you will be given a topic on which to write your essay. This topic is also called a prompt. Write a thesis statement for each of the following prompts.

Prompt 1—Throughout history many important things have been made or invented. Think about an invention that has been important to you. Now write to explain why this one invention has been important.

Thesis statement: _____

_____

_____

_____

Prompt 2—Most people like a certain month or time of year. Think about what you like about a certain month or time of year. Now write to explain why you like this month or time of year.

Thesis statement: _____

_____

_____

_____

Prompt 3—Most people like something in nature, such as plants, animals, or the weather. Think about something in nature and why you like it. Now write to explain why you like this natural thing.

Thesis statement: _____

_____

_____

_____

Prompt 4—Most students learn by listening, reading, or doing. Think about the way you like to learn. Now write to explain why you like to learn this way.

Thesis statement: _____

_____

_____

_____

UNIT 1

Plan and Write Introduction

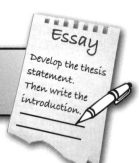
Essay
Develop the thesis statement. Then write the introduction.

① Learn

An **introduction** is an important part of the essay because it introduces the topic of your essay. There are three parts to writing an introduction: the **hook**, the thesis statement, and the three supporting details. The first couple of sentences should hook, or convince the person to read your essay. You may begin your essay with a definition, an interesting fact, or an anecdote (a short story about an interesting or historical incident) to capture the reader's attention.

② Practice

By mastering these components, you will improve your writing and test-taking skills, especially as they relate to the GED Language Arts/Writing Test. Read the paragraph below. Then answer the question that follows.

The reverse triangle, like the one below, represents the introduction of your essay. Start with a broad idea and narrow your focus to "get to the point."

Hook

Thesis Statement

Three Supporting Details

Prompt: Everyone has received advice from a parent, friend, teacher, or co-worker.

Identify one piece of advice that someone has shared with you. Explain when and why the advice was given, how you applied the advice, and whether the advice was valuable. To develop your essay, use your own observations, experiences, and knowledge.

(A)

(1) Many teenagers today do not heed the advice of their parents. (2) Instead, they are more likely to follow advice from a friend or an adult they trust. (3) Last year, I asked Mrs. Morgan, my former social studies teacher, advice on whether or not I should stay with my Uncle Joe and become a plumber. (4) Mrs. Morgan said to me, "Whatever you decide, just make sure you say what you mean." (5) This year, the best advice I have been given is to say what I mean. (6) It helped me make the right decision with my dog Scout, my Uncle Joe, and my future.

✎ WRITING STRATEGIES

When writing your three supporting details, make sure they clearly and obviously support your thesis statement. The thesis statement belongs after the hook, and the supporting details should directly follow the thesis statement.

1. Which of the following sentences contains the three supporting details?

   (1) Instead, they are more likely to follow advice from a friend or an adult they trust.
   (2) Last year, I asked Mrs. Morgan, my former social studies teacher, advice on whether or not I should stay with my Uncle Joe and become a plumber.
   (3) Mrs. Morgan said to me, "Whatever you decide, just make sure you say what you mean."
   (4) This year, the best advice I have been given is to say what I mean.
   (5) It helped me make the right decision with my dog, my Uncle Joe, and my future.

③ **Write**

Directions: On the GED Language Arts/Writing Test, you will be asked to read a prompt and write an essay. Understanding the key components of an introduction will help you produce a strong essay. Below are two sample writing prompts. Write an introductory paragraph for each prompt.

Prompt 1—Throughout history many important things have been made or invented. Think about an invention that has been important to you. Now write to explain why this one invention has been important.

Introduction: _____

_____

_____

_____

_____

_____

_____

_____

_____

_____

_____

Prompt 2—Most people like a certain month or time of year. Think about what you like about a certain month or time of year. Now write to explain why you like this month or time of year.

Introduction: _____

_____

_____

_____

_____

_____

_____

_____

_____

_____

_____

_____

Plan and Write Body

Essay
Develop the thesis statement. Then write the introduction.

① Learn

The **body** of the five-paragraph essay is the writer's opportunity to reintroduce the three supporting details with more explanation. They are the meat and potatoes of the essay. Each paragraph should begin with a **transition**, or a way to move from one idea to the next, and then explain each supporting detail. You will learn more about transitions in Unit 2.

② Practice

By mastering these components, you will improve your writing and test-taking skills, especially as they relate to the GED Language Arts/Writing Test. Read the paragraphs below. Then answer the question that follows.

A Transitions should occur between sentences and paragraphs. Common words or phrases that are used as transitions include:
- In other words
- Although
- In the meantime
- After
- At the same time

B

When using a graphic organizer to structure your essay, each box represents a body paragraph.

WRITING STRATEGIES

Transitions can be used to:
- show time
- give examples
- summarize or conclude
- show place or direction

(B)

(1) **A** <u>After</u> Mrs. Morgan gave me her advice, my girlfriend and I were in the mall shopping for soccer clothes when we passed Jake's Pet Store. (2) In the window was the cutest little beagle. (3) His long, floppy ears and sad brown eyes were pleading to go home with us. (4) It must have been a weak moment for me, because thirty minutes later we were driving home with our dog Scout. (5) I had convinced my girlfriend that I would take care of this puppy. (6) Believe me, I meant what I said. (7) **A** <u>Although</u> it was hard work, I realized Scout depended on me for food and water, a place to sleep, and daily exercise. (8) When our neighbors saw how responsible I was with Scout, they asked me to be their dog walker. (9) Soon I was taking care of half the dogs in the neighborhood.

(C)

(10) It was around this time that my Uncle Joe asked me to go to Little Rock to work with him as a plumber. (11) A couple of summers ago, I stayed with Uncle Joe and worked with him. (12) I wasn't sure what I wanted to do then, so I said I didn't want to go and then changed my mind. (13) I gave him mixed messages. (14) When Uncle Joe asked me this time, I knew what I wanted. (15) I told him I did not want to be a plumber, and just like my promise to my girlfriend about taking care of Scout, I meant what I said.

1. Which of the following sentences is the transition?

(1) Believe me, I meant what I said.
(2) It was around this time that my Uncle Joe asked me to go to Little Rock to work with him as a plumber.
(3) I wasn't sure what I wanted to do then, so I said I didn't want to go and then changed my mind.
(4) I gave him mixed messages.
(5) I told him I did not want to be a plumber, and just like my promise to my girlfriend about taking care of Scout, I meant what I said.

Directions: Read the following writing prompt. Write your thesis statement from page 3 in the space provided. Next, write your first and second supporting details. Then write the first <u>two</u> body paragraphs, making sure you use a transition between each paragraph.

Prompt—Throughout history many important things have been made or invented. Think about an invention that has been important to you. Now write to explain why this one invention has been important.

Thesis statement: _____

_____

_____

Two supporting details:

First: _____

Second: _____

_____

_____

_____

_____

_____

_____

_____

_____

_____

_____

_____

_____

_____

_____

_____

_____

_____

_____

_____

Elaboration of Details

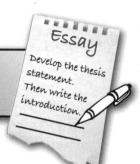

Essay

Develop the thesis statement.
Then write the introduction.

① Learn

To ensure a strong essay, **elaborate** on the given topic. Elaboration can be accomplished by adding details layer by layer. Be sure to explain why your details support the topic of the essay. You can elaborate each supporting detail by using examples, definitions, analogies (when one thing resembles or compares to another), or sequence of events.

② Practice

By mastering this component, you will improve your writing and test-taking skills, especially as they relate to the GED Language Arts/Writing Test. Read the paragraphs below. Then answer the question that follows.

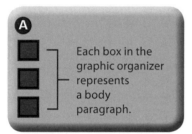

A

Each box in the graphic organizer represents a body paragraph.

B Paragraph C elaborates on the topic of Uncle Joe's work proposition.

One or two sentences is not enough. The following example does not show elaboration: *My Uncle Joe wants me to work with him. I told him I did not want to be a plumber.*

(B)

A (1) After Mrs. Morgan gave me her advice, my girlfriend and I were in the mall shopping for soccer clothes when we passed Jake's Pet Store. (2) In the window was the cutest little beagle. (3) His long, floppy ears and sad brown eyes were pleading to go home with us. (4) It must have been a weak moment for me, because thirty minutes later we were driving home with our dog Scout. (5) I had convinced my girlfriend that I would take care of this puppy. (6) Believe me, I meant what I said. (7) Although it was hard work, I realized Scout depended on me for food and water, a place to sleep, and daily exercise. (8) When our neighbors saw how responsible I was with Scout, they asked me to be their dog walker. (9) Soon I was taking care of half the dogs in the neighborhood.

(C)

A (10) It was around this time that my Uncle Joe asked me to go to Little Rock to work with him as a plumber. (11) A couple of summers ago, I stayed with Uncle Joe and worked with him. (12) I wasn't sure what I wanted to do then, so I said I didn't want to go and then changed my mind. (13) I gave him mixed messages. (14) When Uncle Joe asked me this time, I knew what I wanted. (15) I told him I did not want to be a plumber, and just like my promise to my girlfriend about taking care of Scout, I meant what I said.

✏ WRITING STRATEGIES

When you elaborate on your supporting details in each body paragraph, include the word *because* as a method to provide explanation.

1. Which sentence elaborates on the topic of the "little beagle?"

(1) His long, floppy ears and sad brown eyes were pleading to go home with us.
(2) A couple of summers ago, I stayed with Uncle Joe and worked with him.
(3) I wasn't sure what I wanted to do then, so I said I didn't want to go and then changed my mind.
(4) I gave him mixed messages.
(5) I told him I did not want to be a plumber, and just like my promise to my girlfriend about taking care of Scout, I meant what I said.

③ **Write**

<u>Directions</u>: Read the following writing prompt. Write your thesis statement from page 3 in the space provided. Next, write your third supporting detail. Then write a <u>third</u> body paragraph, using your <u>third</u> supporting detail. Make sure you include the topic, an explanation, and elaboration.

> **Prompt**—Throughout history many important things have been made or invented. Think about an invention that has been important to you. Now write to explain why this one invention has been important.

Thesis statement: _____

_____

_____

One supporting detail:

    Third: _____

_____

_____

_____

_____

_____

_____

_____

_____

_____

_____

_____

_____

_____

_____

_____

UNIT 1

Plan and Write Conclusion

Essay

Develop the thesis statement. Then write the introduction.

① Learn

A **conclusion** is the last impression you leave of your essay. This is your chance to tie up all of the loose ends and sum things up. Connect the concluding paragraph with your introductory paragraph. To accomplish this, try to repeat an idea, word, or phrase, but keep the conclusion simple. Short words and phrases can be powerful when used well. One way to leave a lasting impression is to conclude with an insightful thought or something you've learned in writing this essay.

② Practice

By mastering this component, you will improve your writing and test-taking skills, especially as they relate to the GED Language Arts/Writing Test. Read the paragraph below. Then answer the questions that follow.

The triangle represents your conclusion. Start with a transition. Next, restate the thesis statement using different words. End by giving the reader a bigger picture.

Transition
Restate Thesis
Give the reader the bigger picture

(E)

(1) Throughout this year, I have found Mrs. Morgan's advice to be very valuable. (2) I have said what I meant and followed through with it by doing what I said. (3) I have taken care of my dog and the neighborhood dogs. (4) I told my Uncle Joe that I did not want to be a plumber, and I have decided to become a veterinary assistant. (5) I have learned through these experiences the importance of saying what I mean. (6) Because I have followed Mrs. Morgan's advice, I have gained the respect of my family, community, and even Scout.

WRITING STRATEGIES

DO:
- conclude with a quote
- reference one of your supporting details
- reference books, movies, or pop culture

DON'T:
- apologize
- use the words *I think*
- use exclamation points
- use all caps to emphasize your idea
- just summarize your essay

1. In the above conclusion, how has the writer has chosen to conclude?

   (1) with a quote
   (2) with an insightful thought about his life
   (3) by giving advice
   (4) by apologizing
   (5) by telling how much he likes working with dogs

2. Which of the following sentences restates the thesis?

   (1) Because I have followed Mrs. Morgan's advice, I have gained the respect of my family, community, and even Scout.
   (2) Throughout this year, I have found Mrs. Morgan's advice to be very valuable.
   (3) I have taken care of my dog and the neighborhood dogs.
   (4) I told my Uncle Joe that I did not want to be a plumber, and I have decided to become a veterinary assistant.
   (5) I have learned through these experiences the importance of saying what I mean.

UNIT 1

③ Write

Directions: Read the following writing prompts, and write a conclusion for an essay on each prompt.

> **Prompt 1**—Throughout history many important things have been made or invented. Think about an invention that has been important to you. Now write to explain why this one invention has been important.

_____

_____

_____

_____

_____

_____

_____

_____

_____

_____

_____

> **Prompt 2**—Everyone has responsibilities as they grow older. These may be responsibilities that are related to our personal lives, community, or world. Think about a responsibility you have now or might have in the future. Now write to explain why this responsibility is or will be important in your life.

_____

_____

_____

_____

_____

_____

_____

_____

_____

_____

Review and Revise

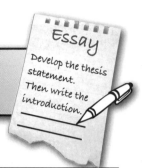

Essay
Develop the thesis statement. Then write the introduction.

1 Learn

Getting a perfect score on the GED essay is not easy, but that is our goal for you. You have only 45 minutes to brainstorm, organize, write, **review**, **revise**, and edit your essay. The good news is that 45 minutes is enough time for you to write your essay because the scorers understand they are reading your rough draft. After you complete your essay, it will be scored on its focus, organization, support, sentence structure, grammar, spelling, punctuation, and word choice. In Units 2-5, you will learn more about the mechanics of editing.

2 Practice

By mastering the skill of revision, you will improve your writing and test-taking skills, especially as they relate to the GED Language Arts/Writing Test. The Essay Checklist and Timing Tips below will help you with your complete essay. To practice revising, read the two paragraphs below. Identify the missing key elements in body paragraph B and rewrite the corrected paragraph B on a separate sheet of paper. Time yourself.

WRITING STRATEGIES

Essay Checklist
- Did you plan your essay using a mental map?
- Do you have a hook?
- Do you have a thesis statement with three supporting details?
- Are all five paragraphs indented?
- Did you use transitions?
- Did you use examples, reasons, facts, or definitions?
- Did you rephrase your thesis statement and three supporting details in your conclusion?
- Did you stay on topic?

Timing Tips

Consider the following timetable to pace yourself as you write.

- 10 minutes to plan your essay
- 30 minutes to write your essay
- 5 minutes to revise and edit your essay

Introduction

Three body paragraphs

Conclusion

Thesis statement: My favorite sport is tennis.
Supporting details: good exercise; I always play with a friend; I like the outfits

(A)
(1) My community center offers a dozen sports to choose from. (2) Last year, I decided to join the tennis class. (3) In the course of a year, tennis has become my favorite sport. (4) I really like tennis because it keeps me healthy, I can play with my friends, and I like the outfits. (5) Tennis isn't an option in a lot of communities, so I was lucky that my rec center offered it.

(B)
(6) Tennis is a great way to stay in shape. (7) During practice, we run laps around the court. (8) Sometimes Coach will make us run if we hit the ball out of bounds.

Write

Directions: Read the following essay. Identify missing key elements and mistakes. Then use the right-hand margin of this page to make the necessary corrections. You may refer to the checklist on page 12 as needed. Paragraph A has been done for you as an example. Time yourself.

Thesis statement: My favorite pastime is going to the dog park.

Supporting details: exercise for my dog; I get to spend time outside; I meet new people.

(A)

It isn't uncommon to see people walking their dogs. A lot of people these days have pets, and many of them are dogs. I have a 5-year-old golden retriever, and I think my favorite pastime is going to the dog park. It is fun because I get to spend quality time outside and meet new people.

(B)

I like to take my dog to the dog park on the weekend for much-needed exercise. I think she really enjoys it, and it keeps her healthy. She also swims because the dog park is big and has a lake. Running and swimming are fun, healthy ways to keep my dog active and healthy.

(C)

My dog isn't the only one that plays at the park. I also like to run around with her. We walk on the hiking trails and spend time soaking up the sun. It's a great way to spend time outdoors. The dog park has trails, tall trees, picnic benches, and a huge lake, so it is a good place to unwind after a long work week.

(D)

Because the dog park is so large, there are many people who visit every day. I am always meeting new people at the park. A guy showed up who looked like my friend Aaron. My dog thought she recognized him and swam over to play. He and his friends started talking to me, and we had a lot in common. It's nice to meet new people so often. Going to the dog park is one of my favorite things to do because my dog and I have lots of fun there. I spend quality time outside and my gets the exercise she needs. We do things that we don't normally do during the work week. I think my dog likes it.

Paragraph A: The introduction is missing a supporting detail. It should be "It is fun because my dog gets to exercise, I get to spend time outside, and I meet new people." Also, the writer uses the words "I think." It should be "My favorite pastime is going to the dog park."

By now you have composed all the parts of a five-paragraph essay on an invention that is important to you. Flip back to pages 5, 7, 9, and 11 to review your introduction, three body paragraphs, and conclusion. Take this time to carefully review what you have written by using the following checklist.

UNIT 1

Introduction:	Yes	No
1) Is the thesis statement clear?	❏	❏
2) Do you have a hook?	❏	❏
3) Do you have three supporting details?	❏	❏
4) Do your supporting details clearly support the thesis statement?	❏	❏
5) Do you stay on topic?	❏	❏

Body Paragraphs:	Yes	No
1) Do you begin each paragraph with a transition?	❏	❏
2) Is each paragraph dedicated to a single supporting detail?	❏	❏
3) Is the supporting detail explained?	❏	❏
4) Do you elaborate?	❏	❏
5) Do you stay on topic?	❏	❏

Conclusion:	Yes	No
1) Is this your fifth paragraph?	❏	❏
2) Do you begin with a transition?	❏	❏
3) Do you restate the thesis statement?	❏	❏
4) Do you rephrase the supporting details?	❏	❏
5) Do you stay on topic?	❏	❏

GED Essay Scoring Rubric

This tool is designed to help readers score an essay. Two scorers read the GED essay, each giving a score between 1 and 4. The average of the two is the final score for the essay portion of the test. The score must be at least 2 to pass the test. Remember that an essay that strays from the given topic receives no score.

4. Effective	**Reader understands and easily follows the writer's expression of ideas.** • presents a clearly focused main idea that addresses the prompt • establishes a clear and logical organizational plan • is coherent with specific details and examples • exhibits varied and precise word choice
3. Adequate	**Reader understands the writer's ideas.** • uses the writing prompt to establish the main idea • uses an identifiable organizational plan • has some focus, but occasionally uneven development; incorporates some specific detail • exhibits appropriate word choice
2. Marginal	**Reader occasionally has difficulty understanding or following the writer's ideas.** • addresses the prompt, though the focus may shift • shows some evidence of an organizational plan • some development, but lacks specific detail; may be limited to a listing, repetitions, or generalizations • exhibits a narrow range of word choice
1. Inadequate	**Reader has difficulty identifying or following the writer's ideas.** • little or no success in establishing a focus • fails to organize ideas • demonstrates little or no development; usually lacks details or examples, or presents irrelevant information • exhibits weak and/or inappropriate words

Directions: If you answered **no** to any of the questions on page 14, rewrite the portions of your essay that need revision in the space provided. Keep the GED Essay Scoring Rubric and checklist in mind while you revise.

Prompt—Throughout history many important things have been made or invented. Think about an invention that has been important to you. Now write to explain why this one invention has been important.

_____

_____

_____

_____

_____

_____

_____

_____

_____

_____

_____

_____

_____

_____

_____

_____

_____

_____

_____

_____

_____

_____

_____

Unit 1 Review

Directions: Read the following prompt, and write an essay on a separate sheet of paper. Use the graphic organizer (mental map) provided to help you brainstorm before you begin writing your essay.

UNIT 1

Prompt 1— Everyone has had a moment in time when he or she was scared. In your essay, identify one time when you have been scared. Explain when and why you were scared, and how you dealt with being scared. To develop your essay, use your own observations, experiences, and knowledge.

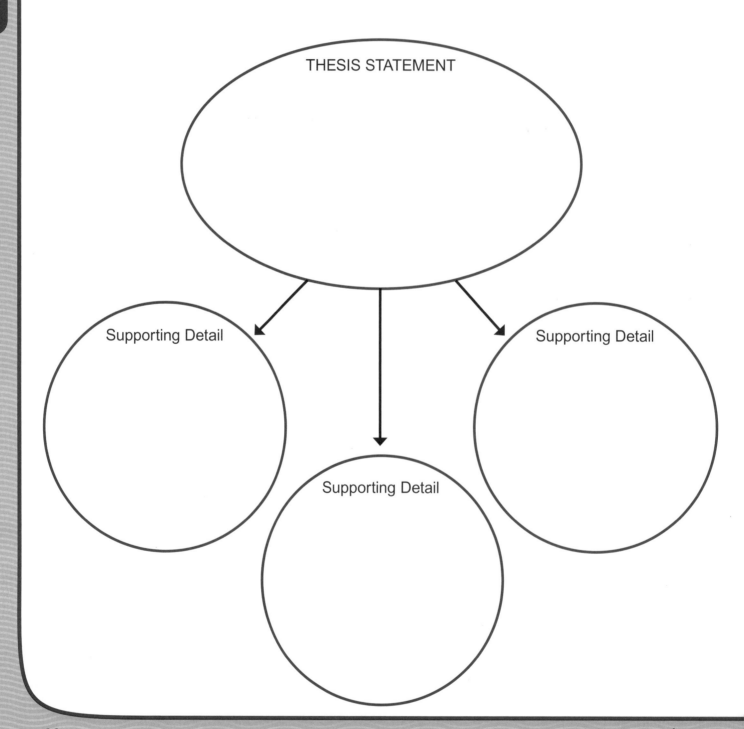

THESIS STATEMENT

Supporting Detail

Supporting Detail

Supporting Detail

Directions: Read the following prompt, and write an essay on a separate sheet of paper. Use the space provided to draw and complete a mental map. This will help you brainstorm before you begin writing your essay.

Prompt 2—Everyone has had a neighbor. In your essay, think about the neighbors you have had. Now write to explain what makes a good neighbor. To develop your essay, use your own observations, experiences, and knowledge.

Directions: Read the following prompt, and write an essay on a separate sheet of paper. Use the space provided to draw and complete a mental map. This will help you brainstorm before you begin writing your essay.

Prompt 3—Everyone has a possession he or she cannot live without. In your essay, identify one indispensible possession. Now write to explain why this possession is indispensible. To develop your essay, use your own observations, experiences, and knowledge.

Directions: Read the following prompt, and write an essay on a separate sheet of paper. Use the space provided to draw and complete a mental map. This will help you brainstorm before you begin writing your essay.

Prompt 4—Everyone has observed someone with good or bad manners. In your essay, identify a time you observed someone with good or bad manners. Explain when and why the manners were good or bad. Now write to explain why having good manners is or is not important. To develop your essay, use your own observations, experiences, and knowledge.

PETER JENNINGS

The Peter Jennings GED Laurel Award Scholarship awards $1,000 annually toward college tuition for exceptional GED recipients.

Peter Jennings was long a trusted guest in living rooms across the United States. As a journalist for ABC News for more than 40 years, Jennings delivered news ranging from the construction of the Berlin Wall in the early 1960s to its fall in the late 1980s. He reported on the civil-rights movement in the United States in the 1960s and on South Africans' struggle against apartheid in the 1980s. He was on the air for more than 60 hours the week of the September 11, 2001, terrorist attacks.

The son of a Canadian radio broadcaster, Jennings began his career at the age of 10, hosting a Saturday morning children's show for the Canadian Broadcasting Company (CBC). He had found his calling. Jennings left school to pursue a career in journalism, earning his GED certificate along the way.

Jennings went to work for ABC News in 1964. Less than a year later, he became the network's youngest news anchor when he hosted *Peter Jennings with the News* (1965 to 1967). Jennings then went abroad and worked as the ABC News bureau chief in Lebanon for seven years. He returned stateside in 1978 to work as a reporter for *World News Tonight*. He became the broadcast's anchor in 1983, a post he held until his death from lung cancer in 2005. He noted,

> **❝I've been there for some of the great moments of the last 30 years. I'm really lucky.❞**

Remembered by many as a trusted name in news, Jennings was also a best-selling author and noted philanthropist who believed in the power of education.

BIO BLAST: Peter Jennings

- Born on July 29, 1938, in Toronto, Ontario
- Authored two well-known books, *The Century* and *In Search of America*
- In 1964, began career with ABC News that lasted more than 40 years
- Anchored the most-watched television event ever, *ABC 2000*, appearing live on camera for 25 hours straight
- Hosted several live news specials for children on topics ranging from AIDS to racial discrimination

Unit 2: Organization

Whether writing a grocery list or performing a job, you are using organization skills in your writing. In Unit 2, you will learn how to more effectively organize your writing by understanding text division and unity within paragraphs. While the GED Language Arts/Writing Test requires a five-paragraph essay, not all written materials need five paragraphs. Take a moment to familiarize yourself with the following glossary of terms, noting the examples provided. These terms will appear throughout the book.

GLOSSARY OF TERMS

Scene: A single setting in which the action occurs. If the writer is telling a story about a new dog, one scene may be at the shelter where the dog is adopted and another at the house that will be the dog's new home. Each scene in the story needs its own paragraph.

Speaker: The narrator of the story or the character being quoted. For example, if you quoted a volunteer at the shelter saying "his favorite toy is a stuffed squirrel," then she would be the speaker. During the remainder of the essay, the writer is the speaker because the story is written from his or her perspective.

Theme: An idea or subject matter that is reflected throughout the essay.

Facts: Information that can be proven true: *the sky is blue*; *people are mammals*.

Statistics: Data that can be expressed in terms of quantity: *According to the Centers for Disease Control and Prevention, unmarried women are less likely to have health insurance.*

Analysis: Identification of a subject or subjects: *After further analysis, it has been proven that gravity pulls objects of different weights at the same rate.*

Phrase: A word or group of words that create a single idea or expression: *A dog is a man's best friend*.

Clause: A group of words that consists of a subject and a verb: *Mary jumps*.

Comma: A punctuation mark that is used within a sentence to represent a pause. Commas are also used to connect clauses, or phrases.

Table of Contents

Text Division

I. Organization
A. Topic
B. Details
C. Transitions

① Learn the Skill

Text division describes a way of organizing text into paragraphs. Each paragraph contains multiple sentences. Because each paragraph contains one idea, be sure to focus on one point at a time. As a writer, begin a new paragraph each time there is a change in idea, scene, time, or speaker. This division also helps you organize an essay into an introduction, body, and conclusion.

② Practice the Skill

By mastering the skill of text division, you will improve your writing and test-taking skills, especially as they relate to the GED Language Arts/Writing Test. Read the paragraphs and strategies below. Then answer the question that follows.

A On the GED Language Arts/ Writing Test, paragraphs are separated with letters within parentheses. However, sometimes the paragraphs are not separated correctly.

B Sentences 1 through 5 describe the author's telephone conversation with Uncle Joe. This text describes one scene and should stand alone in paragraph D. Sentences 6 through 10 give summary information about the advice the author receives from Mrs. Morgan. A change in the text occurs with sentence six. The author shifts from the telephone conversation to reflection. This summary information provides a conclusion for the essay and should stand alone.

(D)

(1) It was time to put my thoughts into action. (2) At the end of the day, I dialed Uncle Joe's telephone number. (3) I told him that I appreciated the offer of work, but I had other plans. (4) I said that I knew that he was probably disappointed, but I would not change my mind. (5) Surprisingly, Uncle Joe said that he understood and that he supported my decision. (6) Although Mrs. Morgan's advice was simple, it was valuable.

(E)

(7) She taught me the importance of matching my words with my thoughts. (8) By following this advice, I gained self-confidence. (9) Now I control my own future by choosing my words carefully. (10) I say what I mean, and I get what I want.

☑ TEST-TAKING TIPS

Draw boxes around blocks of text that describe one scene or one idea, capture a shift in time, or relay the speech of a single character. These boxes will help you visualize where text division should occur and why.

1. Sentence 6: **Although Mrs. Morgan's advice was simple, it was valuable.**

   Which revision should be made to sentence 6?

   (1) move sentence 6 to the beginning of paragraph D
   (2) remove sentence 6
   (3) move sentence 6 to the end of paragraph E
   (4) move sentence 6 to the beginning of paragraph E
   (5) move sentence 6 to follow sentence 1

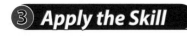

Directions: Choose the <u>one best answer</u> to each question.

<u>Questions 2 through 4</u> refer to the following letter.

Board of Education
Steel School District
405 North Street
Pittsburgh, PA 32589

To Whom It May Concern:

(A)

(1) The purpose of this letter is to persuade you to offer physical education classes on a daily basis in all the district's elementary schools. (2) While I do not negate the importance of content-area subjects, I do not think that you should negate the importance of physical education. (3) The health and well-being of our children are at stake. (4) My first concern is that the schools are not reinforcing the message that physical activity is an essential part of living a healthy life.

(B)

(5) By attending physical education classes one time per week, students learn that physical activity is a hobby rather than a responsibility. (6) The healthcare system in this country bears the burden of adults with this same attitude. (7) My second concern is that the health of the students is at risk due to a lack of physical activity.

(C)

(8) These students spend seven hours per day at school. (9) Yet they are required to be physically active only 45 minutes per week. (10) Just as students need mental exercise to improve their thinking abilities, they need physical exercise to improve the health of their bodies. (11) I know that you do not want the poor health of this district's students to become the next story on the evening news. (12) I urge you to find the funds within the district's budget to offer physical education on a daily basis. (13) Our students deserve an education that has quality, as well as quantity.

Yours Truly,

Eva Rosen

2. Sentence 4: **My first concern is that the schools are not reinforcing the message that physical activity is an essential part of living a healthy life.**

Which revision should be made to the placement of sentence 4?

(1) move sentence 4 to the beginning of paragraph A
(2) remove sentence 4
(3) move sentence 4 to follow sentence 7
(4) move sentence 4 to the beginning of paragraph B
(5) move sentence 4 to the end of paragraph A

3. Sentence 7: **My second concern is that the health of the students is at risk due to a lack of physical activity.**

Which revision should be made to the placement of sentence 7?

(1) remove sentence 7
(2) move sentence 7 to follow sentence 10
(3) move sentence 7 to the beginning of paragraph B
(4) move sentence 7 to follow sentence 3
(5) move sentence 7 to the beginning of paragraph C

4. Sentence 11: **I know that you do not want the poor health of this district's students to become the next story on the evening news.**

Which revision should be made to the placement of sentence 11?

(1) move sentence 11 to begin a new concluding paragraph
(2) remove sentence 11
(3) move sentence 11 to follow sentence 6
(4) move sentence 11 to the beginning of paragraph A
(5) move sentence 11 to the beginning of paragraph C

I. Organization
A. Topic
B. Details
C. Transitions

Topic Sentence

① Learn the Skill

Just as an essay contains an introduction, body, and conclusion, each paragraph within an essay contains these same components. The introduction of a paragraph contains a **topic sentence**. The topic sentence states the subject of the paragraph. Each topic sentence gives more information about the thesis statement of the whole essay and should generally be placed at the beginning of a paragraph.

② Practice the Skill

By mastering the skill of identifying topic sentences, you will improve your writing and test-taking skills, especially as they relate to the GED Language Arts/Writing Test. Read the paragraphs and strategies below. Then answer the question that follows.

A Paragraph E fails to provide a transition from paragraph D. Who is *she*?—Uncle Joe? Remember that each paragraph should contain a topic sentence that relates to the main idea of the essay.

B Paragraph E lacks a topic sentence to unify the ideas presented in the paragraph. The writer also fails to introduce his or her perspective on the topic.

(D)
(1) It was time to put my thoughts into action. (2) At the end of the day, I dialed Uncle Joe's telephone number. (3) I told him that I appreciated his offer of work, but I had other plans. (4) I said that I knew he was probably disappointed, but I would not change my mind. (5) Surprisingly, Uncle Joe said that he understood and that he supported my decision.

(E)
A (6) She taught me the importance of matching my words with my thoughts. (7) By following this advice, I gained self-confidence. (8) Now I control my own future by choosing my words carefully. (9) I say what I mean, and I get what I want.

TEST-TAKING TIPS

Insert each answer choice at the beginning of paragraph E and read the paragraph quietly to yourself. Immediately eliminate answer choices that do not work with the paragraph. For the remaining answer choices, select the one that most clearly states the topic, identifies the writer's perspective on the topic, and unifies the paragraph.

1. Which sentence would be most effective if inserted at the beginning of paragraph E?

   (1) Sticks and stones will break my bones, but words will never hurt me.
   (2) Although Mrs. Morgan's advice was simple, it was valuable.
   (3) Say what you mean, and mean what you say.
   (4) Intention is a powerful tool in creating the life that you want.
   (5) Mrs. Morgan said that self-confidence is an important aspect of goal-setting.

Directions: Choose the one best answer to each question.

Questions 2 through 4 refer to the following information.

Texas Voter Registration Forms

(A)

(1) Potential voters must be citizens of the United States. (2) They must also be at least 18 years old. (3) Voters must also have identification, such as driver's licenses or social security numbers. (4) Additionally, potential voters may not have any pending felony convictions or compromised mental statuses.

(B)

(5) Potential voters may find registration forms online or at public establishments, such as post offices or libraries. (6) The registration forms must be filed in the states and counties where voters live. (7) Completed forms can be mailed to the appropriate government agency in each state. (8) Registrations become active within 30 days of receipt.

(C)

(9) Potential voters must provide their names and addresses. (10) In addition, they must record their birthdays, genders, and identification numbers. (11) Finally, voters must respond to several questions regarding citizenship and criminal convictions. (12) All voter registration forms must be signed and dated.

---

2. Which sentence would be most effective if inserted at the beginning of paragraph A?

   (1) Voting is a democratic responsibility that all Americans should fulfill.
   (2) Many groups of Americans had to fight for the right to vote.
   (3) There are several qualifications for voting in the United States.
   (4) Voting is a privilege that all Americans should respect.
   (5) The required age for voting should be lowered to 16.

3. Which sentence would be most effective if inserted at the beginning of paragraph B?

   (1) Internet access provides U.S. citizens with the opportunity to fulfill civic responsibilities.
   (2) Voter registration should be nationalized so that voters do not need to re-register when they move.
   (3) Post offices serve several important functions within American culture.
   (4) Voter registration forms are easy to obtain and file.
   (5) Libraries serve important cultural functions within a society.

4. Which sentence would be most effective if inserted at the beginning of paragraph C?

   (1) Voter registration forms must be typed or printed.
   (2) Make sure to check all the boxes on the form or it will be returned.
   (3) Convicted felons may appeal to have their voting rights restored.
   (4) Voter registration forms are long and complicated.
   (5) The voter registration form is simple and requires only minimal information.

UNIT 2

Supporting Details

I. Organization
A. Topic
B. Details
C. Transitions

① Learn the Skill

The body of a paragraph contains details that support the topic sentence. You learned about the basics of supporting details in Unit 1. Now you can learn to apply that knowledge to individual paragraphs. As you may recall, **supporting details** may include facts, statistics, examples, or analysis. The conclusion of a paragraph emphasizes the connection between the topic sentence and the supporting details.

② Practice the Skill

By mastering the skill of identifying supporting details, you will improve your writing and test-taking skills, especially as they relate to the GED Language Arts/Writing Test. Read the paragraph and strategies below. Then answer the question that follows.

A The first sentence of the paragraph is the topic sentence: "Mrs Morgan was right, I needed to say no and mean it."

B The supporting details that follow the topic sentence should provide explanation. However, an additional detail where the _____ cue is placed would offer a more insightful explanation of the conflict.

(C)

(1) <u>Mrs. Morgan was right, I needed to say no and mean it</u>. (2) Uncle Joe wanted me to move to Little Rock to work for him in his plumbing shop. (3) I had said "No" to his previous requests, but he kept pushing the issue. (4) I'm sure that he remembered the time that I told him I didn't want to spend three weeks with him and Aunt Mary during my summer vacation. (5) __ _____ (6) I'd said "No" and then changed my mind a dozen times in response to Uncle Joe's requests. (7) He had no reason to think that this time would be any different.

TEST-TAKING TIPS

First, identify the topic, or main idea, of the paragraph. The narrator is experiencing a conflict over saying what he or she means and sticking with it. Now, identify the answer choice that gives readers supporting information regarding this idea.

1. Which sentence would be most effective if inserted as sentence 5 in paragraph C?

   (1) However, I let my uncle talk me into making the visit, and I ended up having a great time.
   (2) I enjoyed working for Uncle Joe during my vacation.
   (3) Uncle Joe took care of my mother when she was little, so he takes a special interest in my life because I am my mother's child.
   (4) It is important to respect one's elders, so I needed to do what Uncle Joe asked.
   (5) Uncle Joe and Aunt Mary live in Little Rock, which is about a two-hour drive from my house.

UNIT 2

Directions: Choose the <u>one best answer</u> to each question.

Questions 2 through 4 refer to the following information.

How to Plan a Vacation

(A)
(1) Summer is approaching, and it's time to start thinking about planning a family vacation. (2) There are three things to consider when planning a vacation: interests, money, and time.

(B)
(3) First, identify who will be going on the vacation. (4) Then take a survey of interests. (5) Do the participants enjoy water sports, hiking, or visiting museums? (6) Make sure to ask the participants to share ongoing interests, as well as new interests.
(7) _____
(8) Once you have determined these interests, you can select two or three possible destinations. (9) Finally, research the attractions and sites at each of these destinations.

(C)
(10) One consideration in deciding upon the final destination is money. (11) How much money does the family want to spend on the trip? (12) _____
_____
(13) Remember that a vacation is possible with almost any budget in mind. (14) Next, you should prepare a budget for each possible destination. (15) Make sure to include travel expenses, such as airplane tickets or gasoline. (16) You also need to include food and lodging. (17) Don't forget to include entertainment expenses as well.

(D)
(18) One final consideration is time. (19) How much time does the family have for the vacation, and how much time does the family want to devote to travel? (20) Some people think that travel is part of the experience of a vacation. (21) _____
_____
(22) Time can also impact the budget. (23) For example, a destination closer to home may cut down on travel expenses and allow the family more time at the destination.

---

2. Which sentence would be most effective if inserted as sentence 7 in paragraph B?

   (1) Too many vacationers mean too many competing interests.
   (2) Participants often enjoy visiting unusual places.
   (3) Another option is to vacation at home by finding out what's new in your city.
   (4) For example, one participant may enjoy visiting beaches, but he would also like to learn how to fish.
   (5) Vacations have many health benefits for workaholics, because they relieve stress and improve family relationships.

3. Which sentence would be most effective if inserted as sentence 12 in paragraph C?

   (1) Choose a figure that will not cause stress for the family.
   (2) Most people end up going over budget on a vacation.
   (3) There are better ways for a family to spend its money than a vacation.
   (4) Consult a financial advisor before planning a vacation.
   (5) It's best to save for a vacation a year in advance.

4. Which sentence would be most effective if inserted as sentence 21 in paragraph D?

   (1) Make sure to budget your time as well as your money.
   (2) Make sure that all family members have watches to help you stay on a vacation schedule.
   (3) Others feel annoyed by time spent traveling.
   (4) Convince your family that the journey is more important than the destination.
   (5) High gas prices prevent long trips.

UNIT 2

Transitions

I. Organization
A. Topic
B. Details
C. Transitions

① Learn the Skill

You learned about the basics of transitions in Unit 1. Now you can learn to apply that knowledge to individual paragraphs. As a writer develops the sentences in a paragraph to state the topic and offer supporting details, he or she must also show the connections between ideas through the use of **transitions**. As you may recall, transitions are words and phrases that show connections, such as time, direction, similarity, or difference. Transitional words and phrases are generally placed at the beginning of a sentence and followed by a comma.

② Practice the Skill

By mastering the skill of identifying transitions, you will improve your writing and test-taking skills, especially as they relate to the GED Language Arts/Writing Test. Read the paragraph and strategies below. Then answer the question that follows.

Ⓐ Notice that there is a contrast between the time the advice is given by Mrs. Morgan and the time period of the narrative. The writer is telling about events that happened in the past. A transitional phrase will help the writer show this contrast between time periods.

Ⓑ The paragraph is missing transitions. Think about the transitions you might use in paragraph A. The following transitions are examples that show contrast: *although, but, despite, however, in contrast, on the other hand, nevertheless,* and *yet.*

(A)
(1) "When you say no, mean it," Mrs. Morgan, my former U.S. History teacher, laughed as she brushed a strand of reddish-blond hair from her eyes. (2) We were standing together in the hallway outside one wing of my old school. (3) The warm afternoon sun kept us from other obligations. (4) "That's one thing I always tried to do with my kids. (5) I didn't want to send the message that I didn't mean what I said. (6) If people think you don't mean what you say, they will take advantage of you," she finished, giving me a motherly look. (7) This piece of advice would change my life in a positive way.

☑ TEST-TAKING TIPS

Make each change to the sentence. Then read the sentence aloud or say it in your head. Remember to pause for one beat when you encounter a comma. Choose the answer choice that clearly establishes a connection between ideas.

1. Sentence 7: **This piece of advice would change my life in a positive way.**

   Which correction should be made to sentence 7?

   (1) insert a comma after <u>advice</u>
   (2) remove <u>in a positive way</u>
   (3) insert <u>Although I didn't know it at the time,</u> before <u>This</u>
   (4) insert <u>in other words,</u> before <u>change</u>
   (5) no correction is necessary

 **Apply the Skill**

Directions: Choose the <u>one best answer</u> to each question.

<u>Questions 2 through 4</u> refer to the following information.

Dress for Success

(A)
(1) Whether you're going to a job interview, work, or a social gathering, your appearance matters. (2) The old saying is true: "You never get a second chance to make a first impression." (3) The next time you find yourself staring into your closet wondering what to wear, consider these tips.

(B)
(4) Wear clothes that are clean, simple, neat, and conservative. (5) You want to match the environment. (6) If others will be wearing suits, then you should wear a suit. (7) If others will be wearing dress shoes, then wear dress shoes. (8) Your attire tells people that you care about the environment, the function, and those around you.

(C)
(9) Your hairstyle and fingernails should also be clean and neat. (10) Choose a conservative hairstyle that is flattering to your face. (11) Both men and women should consider getting a manicure. (12) Clean, well-groomed hands suggest attention to detail. (13) Women should stay away from bright or unusual polish colors. (14) Choose something pretty and subtle.

(D)
(15) When choosing accessories, understatement is the key. (16) Do not wear too much jewelry, cologne, or perfume. (17) Too much jewelry is gaudy. (18) Too much scent may cause discomfort to those around you. (19) Do not chew gum or suck on mints, but make sure that your mouth is clean and your breath fresh. (20) Gum or mints are distracting, as is bad breath. (21) A winning smile will attract others to you.

---

2. Sentence 6: **If others will be wearing suits, then you should wear a suit.**

   Which is the best way to write the underlined portion of sentence 6? If the original is the best way, choose option (1).

   (1) If others
   (2) For example, if others
   (3) Although, if others
   (4) Afterward, if others
   (5) Otherwise, if others

3. Sentences 12 and 13: **Clean, well-groomed hands suggest attention to detail. Women should stay away from bright or unusual polish colors.**

   Which is the most effective revision of sentences 12 and 13?

   (1) Even though clean, well-groomed hands suggest attention to detail, women should stay away from bright or unusual polish colors, and men should too.
   (2) Beyond this, clean, well-groomed hands suggest attention to detail. Women should stay away from bright or unusual polish colors.
   (3) Clean, well-groomed hands suggest attention to detail. Nearby, women should stay away from bright or unusual polish colors.
   (4) Clean, well-groomed hands suggest attention to detail. However, women should stay away from bright or unusual polish colors.
   (5) no correction is necessary

4. Sentence 21: **A winning smile will attract others to you.**

   Which word or phrase would be most effective if inserted at the beginning of sentence 21?

   (1) In contrast,
   (2) In the same manner,
   (3) Also,
   (4) Similarly,
   (5) Likewise,

Unity and Coherence

I. Organization
A. Topic
B. Details
C. Transitions

① Learn the Skill

Unity and **coherence** are established in a paragraph when one sentence flows smoothly and logically to the next, when all sentences relate to the topic sentence, and when there are no unnecessary or irrelevant details. Unity and coherence can be achieved through the full development of an idea. As a writer, you can also convey unity and coherence using varied but complementary sentence structure, as well as consistency in point of view and usage. You will learn more about sentence structure in Unit 3.

② Practice the Skill

By mastering the skill of identifying unity and coherence, you will improve your writing and test-taking skills, especially as they relate to the GED Language Arts/Writing Test. Read the paragraph and strategies below. Then answer the question that follows.

A The topic sentence states that Mrs. Morgan's advice was valuable. All of the remaining sentences should relate to this topic.

B Any sentence that does not relate to the topic is unnecessary or irrelevant and should be removed. Carefully read the paragraph, checking to see if the sentences stay on topic.

(E)
(1) Although Mrs. Morgan's advice was simple, <u>it was valuable</u>. (2) She taught me the importance of matching my words with my thoughts. (3) By following this advice, I gained self-confidence. (4) Any expert in psychology will agree that self-confidence is an important aspect of one's self-esteem. (5) Now I control my own future by choosing my words carefully. (6) I say what I mean, and I get what I want.

☑ **TEST-TAKING TIPS**

When examining a paragraph for unity and coherence, underline the topic sentence. Then, draw an arrow to the topic sentence from each sentence that relates to the topic sentence. Any sentence without an arrow needs to be revised or removed.

1. Sentence 4: **Any expert in psychology will agree that self-confidence is an important aspect of one's self-esteem.**

   Which revision should be made to the placement of sentence 4?

   (1) remove sentence 4
   (2) move sentence 4 to the beginning of paragraph E
   (3) move sentence 4 to follow sentence 2
   (4) move sentence 4 to the end of paragraph E
   (5) no correction is necessary

Directions: Choose the one best answer to each question.

Questions 2 through 4 refer to the following information.

Saving Water

(A)
(1) Where is most of the water used in your home? (2) You're right! (3) If you want to conserve water, the bathroom is the place to begin. (4) A new showerhead or toilet may save one to five gallons per use. (5) Fix leaks to toilets, showers, and sinks immediately. (6) You may save up to 200 gallons per day. (7) Also, replace older fixtures with new water-saving fixtures. (8) Finally, change your habits. (9) Short showers can result in reduced water bills.

(B)
(10) Now, let's move to the next culprit in the crime of water wasting—the kitchen. (11) Many of the same tips that work in your bathroom work in the kitchen, too. (12) For example, you can install water-saving faucets and dishwashers. (13) In addition, don't double wash dishes by rinsing them and then running them through the dishwasher. (14) Just put dishes in the dishwasher and wash only full loads. (15) This practice saves water and the amount of time you spend doing the dishes. (16) It is well known that people do not enjoy doing household chores such as dishes.

(C)
(17) Now, let's apply these same ideas to your laundry room. (18) What's good for the dishwasher is good for the clothes washer. (19) Wash only full loads, and replace older washer models with new water-saving models. (20) If you follow these tips, your next decision will be what to do with the money you save on your water bill. (21) Consider saving this money in a vacation account for a trip to one of the nation's beautiful bodies of water. (22) In a short amount of time, you and your family may find yourself enjoying the Pacific Ocean as you lie on one of California's sunny beaches.

---

2. Sentence 4: **A new showerhead or toilet may save one to five gallons per use.**

   Which revision should be made to the placement of sentence 4?

   (1) move sentence 4 to the beginning of paragraph A
   (2) move sentence 4 to the beginning of paragraph B
   (3) move sentence 4 to the end of paragraph A
   (4) move sentence 4 to follow sentence 7
   (5) no correction is necessary

3. Sentence 16: **It is well known that people do not enjoy doing household chores such as dishes.**

   Which revision should be made to the placement of sentence 16?

   (1) move sentence 16 to the end of paragraph C
   (2) remove sentence 16
   (3) move sentence 16 to the beginning of paragraph B
   (4) move sentence 16 to follow sentence 14
   (5) no correction is necessary

4. Sentence 22: **In a short amount of time, you and your family may find yourself enjoying the Pacific Ocean as you lie on one of California's sunny beaches.**

   Which revision should be made to the placement of sentence 22?

   (1) move sentence 22 to the beginning of paragraph A
   (2) move sentence 22 to the beginning of paragraph C
   (3) remove sentence 22
   (4) move sentence 22 to follow sentence 20
   (5) no correction is necessary

The Unit Review is structured to resemble the GED Language Arts/Writing Test. Be sure to read each question and all possible answers very carefully before choosing your answer.

To record your answers, fill in the numbered circle that corresponds to the answer you select for each question in the Unit Review.

Do not rest your pencil on the answer area while considering your answer. Make no stray or unnecessary marks. If you change an answer, erase your first mark completely.

Mark only one answer space for each question; multiple answers will be scored as incorrect.

Sample Question

Sentence 6: **Lastly, chop a mixture of fruits into bite-sized pieces and place the pieces in a high-powered blender.**

Which correction should be made to sentence 6?

(1) remove <u>Lastly</u>
(2) move sentence 6 to the beginning of paragraph A
(3) change <u>Lastly</u> to <u>Finally</u>
(4) move sentence 6 to the end of paragraph D
(5) no correction is necessary

● ② ③ ④ ⑤

<u>Directions</u>: Choose the <u>one best answer</u> to each question.

<u>Questions 1 through 6</u> refer to the following information.

A Smooth Meal Replacement

(A)

(1) Many experts caution dieters against liquid calories. (2) Also, a smoothie is a good alternative to a traditional meal. (3) With some fruit and a blender, you can easily add valuable nutrients to your diet and keep your calories under control. (4) Begin by gathering your favorite fruits, such as strawberries, bananas, or blueberries.

(B)

(5) Also consider exotic fruits such as mangoes or pineapples. (6) Chop a mixture of fruits into bite-sized pieces and place the pieces in a high-powered blender.

(C)

(7) Choose your favorite juice. (8) Make sure that you use a brand that contains 100% fruit juice with no added sugars. (9) You can also choose to use low fat or skim milk. (10) Add a splash of liquid to the blender along with a couple of handfuls of crushed ice.

(D)

(11) You may choose to add supplements such a protein powder, vitamins, or herbs. (12) _____

_____

(13) You can add a teaspoon of each to the blender. (14) Therefore, blend the ingredients into a smooth, fruity concoction. (15) You may alter your blending time depending on whether you like chunks of fruit in your smoothie.

1. Sentence 2: **<u>Also</u>, a smoothie is a good alternative to a traditional meal.**

   Which is the best way to write the underlined portion of sentence 2? If the original is the best way, choose option (1).

   (1) Also
   (2) Furthermore
   (3) In addition
   (4) However
   (5) In other words

   ① ② ③ ④ ⑤

2. Sentence 4: **Begin by gathering your favorite fruits, such as strawberries, bananas, or blueberries.**

   Which revision should be made to the placement of sentence 4?

   (1) move sentence 4 to the beginning of paragraph B
   (2) remove sentence 4
   (3) move sentence 4 to the beginning of paragraph A
   (4) move sentence 4 to follow sentence 1
   (5) no correction is necessary

   ① ② ③ ④ ⑤

3. Which sentence would be most effective if inserted at the beginning of paragraph C?

   (1) Many fruit juices contain added sugar.
   (2) Cutting the fat out of milk is a good way to reduce liquid calories.
   (3) Fill the remainder of the blender with ice.
   (4) Next, you'll need a liquid.
   (5) Use whole milk if you're making the smoothie for a small child.

   ① ② ③ ④ ⑤

4. Sentence 11: **You may choose to add supplements such a protein powder, vitamins, or herbs.**

   Which word or phrase would be most effective if inserted at the beginning of sentence 11?

   (1) In contrast,
   (2) Finally,
   (3) In the same manner,
   (4) Similarly,
   (5) Likewise,

   ① ② ③ ④ ⑤

5. Which sentence would be most effective if inserted as sentence 12 in paragraph D?

   (1) Supplements help enhance nutrition.
   (2) Many people do not get enough important nutrients in their daily diets.
   (3) These items are available in any health food store.
   (4) Meat is another source of protein.
   (5) Fruit contains a variety of vitamins.

   ① ② ③ ④ ⑤

6. Sentence 14: **<u>Therefore</u>, blend the ingredients into a smooth, fruity concoction.**

   Which is the best way to write the underlined portion of sentence 14? If the original is the best way, choose option (1).

   (1) Therefore
   (2) However
   (3) Then
   (4) In contrast
   (5) Although

   ① ② ③ ④ ⑤

Directions: Choose the <u>one best answer</u> to each question.

<u>Questions 7 through 12</u> refer to the following information.

Paint for Change

(A)
(1) One simple and relatively inexpensive way to redecorate a room is to give it a paint job. (2) Nothing changes a room or cleans it up like a new coat of paint. (3) You can also purchase new accessories, such as pillows and rugs. (4) Follow these tips to transform a room and the life you live in that room. (5) First, choose several possible paint colors based on your home and the furniture and accessories you plan to use in the room.

(B)
(6) Remember that darker colors tend to make a room look smaller. (7) Pick up color swatches at a local paint store. (8) Tape the swatches to a wall in the room for several days so that you can consider these color options before making a final selection.

(C)
(9) You will need to purchase paint, primer, spackle, rollers, pans, brushes, a putty knife, and tape. (10) You will also need a step ladder, drop cloths, and several rags.

(D)
(11) Finally, it's time to prepare the room. (12) Unfortunately, it usually takes longer to prepare a room than to paint it. (13) _____

_____
(14) Spackle any holes that need patching. (15) Tape the perimeter of the room at the floor and ceiling levels, along with any trim around windows and doors. (16) Move furniture away from walls and cover with drop cloths. (17) You want to put tape anywhere that you don't want to put paint.

---

7. Sentence 3: **You can also purchase new accessories, such as pillows and rugs.**

   Which revision should be made to the placement of sentence 3?

   (1) move sentence 3 to the beginning of paragraph A
   (2) move sentence 3 to follow sentence 1
   (3) remove sentence 3
   (4) move sentence 3 to the end of paragraph A
   (5) no correction is necessary

   ①②③④⑤

8. Sentence 5: **First, choose several possible paint colors based on your home and the furniture and accessories you plan to use in the room.**

   Which revision should be made to the placement of sentence 5?

   (1) move sentence 5 to the beginning of paragraph B
   (2) move sentence 5 to the end of paragraph B
   (3) move sentence 5 to follow sentence 7
   (4) remove sentence 5
   (5) no correction is necessary

   ①②③④⑤

9. Which sentence would be most effective if inserted at the beginning of paragraph C?

   (1) You need a step ladder to reach high places.
   (2) Next, gather supplies and tools for the job.
   (3) Drop clothes will keep paint splatter from staining the flooring.
   (4) If you plan to change paint colors, roll on a coat of primer first.
   (5) Blue painter's tape is best, but you can also use masking tape.

   ①②③④⑤

10. Sentence 11: **<u>Finally</u>, it's time to prepare the room.**

    Which is the best way to write the underlined portion of sentence 11? If the original is the best way, choose option (1).

    (1) Finally
    (2) First
    (3) Second
    (4) In conclusion
    (5) Similarly

    ①②③④⑤

11. Which sentence would be most effective if inserted as sentence 13 in paragraph D?

    (1) Roll the paint on the walls in a thick, even coat.
    (2) Use a brush to apply paint near ceilings and baseboards.
    (3) Make sure that the room is well ventilated.
    (4) Plan several hours to complete a painting project.
    (5) Remove window treatments and pictures from the walls.

    ①②③④⑤

12. Sentence 16: **Move furniture away from walls and cover with drop cloths.**

    Which revision should be made to the placement of sentence 16?

    (1) move sentence 16 to the beginning of paragraph B
    (2) move sentence 16 to the beginning of paragraph D
    (3) move sentence 16 to follow sentence 10
    (4) move sentence 16 to before sentence 14
    (5) no correction is necessary

    ①②③④⑤

UNIT 2

Directions: Choose the <u>one best answer</u> to each question.

<u>Questions 13 through 18</u> refer to the following information.

How to Buy a Digital Camera

(A)
(1) If you haven't joined the digital camera craze, you may be feeling a little out of touch as you drop off film at the drug store and come back a few days later to pick up your photographs. (2) The prospect of buying a digital camera may seem confusing. (3) You may find yourself wondering, *What's a megapixel anyway, and how many do I need?* (4) Lastly, the following information will bring the task of purchasing a digital camera into focus.

(B)
(5) More megapixels mean better quality images. (6) If you want to print the same type of images that you're picking up at the drug store, then you need four or five megapixels. (7) You need to consider the cost of more megapixels with regard to your budget. (8) If you plan to exchange photographs with others electronically, then two megapixels will do the job. (9) If you like to take close shots of flowering plants or sticky-faced children, you will want to get a camera with an optical zoom.

(C)
(10) With this feature, you can get clear images without sacrificing drug-store quality prints.

(D)
(11) A camera with a lot of memory can hold more pictures at one time. (12) Once the memory card is full, you have to transfer or delete pictures before you can take more pictures. (13) Note, however, that you can buy and add memory cards to most cameras to increase capacity.

---

13. Sentence 2: **<u>The prospect</u> of buying a digital camera may seem confusing.**

Which is the best way to write the underlined portion of sentence 2? If the original is the best way, choose option (1).

(1) The prospect
(2) Understandably, the prospect
(3) Afterward, the prospect
(4) Otherwise, the prospect
(5) For example, the prospect

① ② ③ ④ ⑤

14. Sentence 4: **<u>Lastly</u>, the following information will bring the task of purchasing a digital camera into focus.**

Which is the best way to write the underlined portion of sentence 4? If the original is the best way, choose option (1).

(1) Lastly
(2) Hopefully
(3) Finally
(4) Therefore
(5) On the other hand

① ② ③ ④ ⑤

15. Sentence 7: **You need to consider the cost of more megapixels with regard to your budget.**

Which revision should be made to the placement of sentence 7?

(1) move sentence 7 to the beginning of paragraph B
(2) move sentence 7 to follow sentence 8
(3) remove sentence 7
(4) move sentence 7 to the end of paragraph C
(5) no correction is necessary

① ② ③ ④ ⑤

16. Sentence 9: **If you like to take close shots of flowering plants or sticky-faced children, you will want to get a camera with an optical zoom.**

Which revision should be made to the placement of sentence 9?

(1) move sentence 9 to the beginning of paragraph B
(2) remove sentence 9
(3) move sentence 9 to follow sentence 10
(4) move sentence 9 to the beginning of paragraph C
(5) no correction is necessary

① ② ③ ④ ⑤

17. Which sentence would be most effective if inserted at the beginning of paragraph D?

(1) One result of aging is the loss of memory.
(2) You should download and organize the images from a digital camera on a regular basis.
(3) A digital camera allows you to delete poor images.
(4) In choosing a digital camera, you should weigh your needs against your budget.
(5) If you are relying on your new digital camera to store your memories, you'll want to get a camera with a lot of memory.

① ② ③ ④ ⑤

18. Sentence 13: **Note, <u>however</u>, that you can buy and add memory cards to most cameras to increase capacity.**

Which is the best way to write the underlined portion of sentence 13? If the original is the best way, choose option (1).

(1) however
(2) finally
(3) therefore
(4) lastly
(5) for example

① ② ③ ④ ⑤

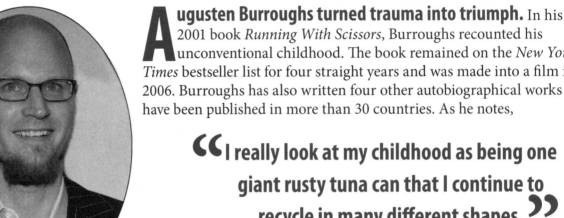

GED JOURNEYS

AUGUSTEN BURROUGHS

Augusten Burroughs turned trauma into triumph. In his 2001 book *Running With Scissors*, Burroughs recounted his unconventional childhood. The book remained on the *New York Times* bestseller list for four straight years and was made into a film in 2006. Burroughs has also written four other autobiographical works that have been published in more than 30 countries. As he notes,

> **"I really look at my childhood as being one giant rusty tuna can that I continue to recycle in many different shapes."**

Although Burroughs had no formal education beyond elementary school, he earned his GED certificate and began a more than 17-year career in advertising. However, struggles with alcoholism nearly cost him his life. The turning point came as Burroughs neared completion of his first novel, *Sellevision*. Burroughs wrote the book in just seven days, during which time he stopped drinking. He has remained sober since.

In addition to working on his next book, Burroughs regularly speaks at colleges and universities. The range of topics he explores includes sexual abuse, alcoholism, writing, and humor. He lives in western Massachusetts and New York City with his partner and their dogs.

In addition to writing best-sellers, Burroughs also takes time to speak at prestigious literary festivals around the world.

BIO BLAST: Augusten Burroughs

- Born October 23, 1965, in Pittsburgh, Pennsylvania
- Experienced a turbulent childhood that provided the basis for his 2001 book *Running With Scissors*
- Overcame alcoholism to become a noted author
- Honored twice by *Entertainment Weekly* as one of the 25 funniest people in America

Sentence Structure

Unit 3: Sentence Structure

Structure is as important to writing as it is to buildings. Without a sound structure, a building may fall apart. The same is true when you write. In Unit 3, you will practice techniques that will provide the tools you need to build strong sentences. Take a moment to familiarize yourself with the following glossary of terms, noting the examples provided. These terms will appear throughout the book.

GLOSSARY OF TERMS

Verb: The action or state of being: *Mary jumps rope.*

Subject: The person or thing doing the action: *Mary jumps rope.*

Punctuation: Marks that provide structure within written text, such as periods (.), commas (,), semicolons (;), quotation marks (" "), question marks (?), exclamation points (!), dashes (–), and hyphens (-).

Coordinating conjunction: Words that combine two items of equal importance in regards to the rules of sentence structure: *for, and, nor, but, or, yet,* and *so.*

Independent clause: A sentence or clause that can stand alone: *That is why the bagels were cold.*

Dependent clause: A clause that is dependent on another clause, or group of words, and cannot stand alone: *That is why the bagels were cold.*

Adverb: Any word that modifies a verb, an adjective, or another adverb: *A deliciously ripe apple fell quickly from the tree.*

Conjunctive adverb: An adverb that generally shows cause and effect, sequence, contrast and comparison, and connects two clauses: *also, that is, so, therefore.* (It was snowing, so I was cold).

Subordinating conjunctions: A conjunction that introduces dependent clauses: *if, so that, because.*

Adjective: A word that modifies or describes a noun or pronoun: *red, fast, pretty, new, old.*

Table of Contents

Complete Sentences

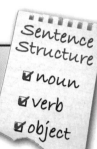

Sentence
Structure
☑ noun
☑ verb
☑ object

① Learn the Skill

Effective writing is dependent on **complete sentences**. A sentence is complete when it contains the following elements: subject, verb, complete idea, and end punctuation. The subject identifies who or what the sentence describes. The verb identifies the subject's state of existence or how the subject acts. A complete idea stands alone without other phrases or clauses. All sentences end with punctuation, such as a period, exclamation point, or question mark. You will learn more about verbs and punctuation in Units 4 and 5.

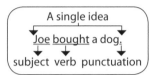

A single idea

Joe bought a dog.

subject verb punctuation

② Practice the Skill

By mastering the skill of understanding complete sentences, you will improve your writing and test-taking skills, especially as they relate to the GED Language Arts/Writing Test. Read the paragraph and strategies below. Then answer the question that follows.

A Sentence 4 has a subject (*he*), an action (*kept pushing*), and an endmark (.).

B However, sentence 4 is not a complete sentence because it begins with the conjunction *but*. This conjunction suggests that sentence 4 needs to be attached to sentence 3 to complete the idea.

(C)

(1) Mrs. Morgan was right; I needed to say no and mean it. (2) Uncle Joe wanted me to move to Little Rock to work for him in his plumbing shop. (3) I had said "No" to his previous requests. (4) <u>But he kept pushing the issue</u>. (5) I'm sure he remembered the time I told him that I didn't want to spend three weeks with him and Aunt Mary during my vacation. (6) However, I had let my uncle talk me into making the visit, and I ended up having a great time. (7) I'd said "No" and then changed my mind a dozen times in response to Uncle Joe's requests. (8) He had no reason to think that this time would be any different.

✓ TEST-TAKING TIPS

Generally, a complete sentence should not begin with a coordinating conjunction such as *and*, *but*, or *or*. If you see a coordinating conjunction at the beginning of a sentence, check to make sure that the sentence is complete.

1. Sentences 3 and 4: **I had said "No" to his previous requests. But he kept pushing the issue.**

   Which is the best way to write the underlined portion of sentences 3 and 4? If the original is the best way, choose option (1).

   (1) requests. But
   (2) requests, but
   (3) requests, and
   (4) requests. Or
   (5) requests? But

Directions: Choose the <u>one best answer</u> to each question.

<u>Questions 2 through 5</u> refer to the following information.

Form a Book Club

(A)

(1) One of the great joys of reading a good book comes after the final page is read and the covers shut. (2) Readers often want to share the experience of a book with fellow readers by discussing various aspects of a book. (3) Here's how to join this literary movement and start a club of your own.

(B)

(4) First, invite all your book-loving friends to a start-up meeting. (5) At this first gathering, establish a regular meeting time for a monthly meeting. (6) Such as the third Wednesday of every month at 7:00 P.M.

(C)

(7) Additionally, create the rules of the group. (8) Consider how the meeting locations will rotate. (9) Will you move from the home of one member to the home of another member in a designated sequence (10) Will you meet at a local coffee house? (11) What sorts of refreshments are expected at each meeting, and who provides them? (12) Does each member bring a healthy snack to share pot-luck style?

(D)

(13) Think about what books will be selected and how the books will be selected. (14) Focus on fiction, classics, self-help books, or some combination of genres? (15) Will the host of each meeting choose the book? (16) Will members each contribute titles for a lottery drawing?

(E)

(17) Gather input regarding the format for discussions. (18) For instance, does the group want the host to use prepared questions to lead the discussion? (19) Does each member want to contribute one question for discussion at each meeting?

---

2. Sentence 6: **Such as the third Wednesday of every month at 7:00 P.M.**

   Which correction should be made to sentence 6?

   (1) replace <u>Such</u> with <u>, such</u>
   (2) insert a comma after <u>month</u>
   (3) insert a period after <u>month</u>
   (4) remove <u>Such as</u>
   (5) no correction is necessary

3. Sentence 9: **Will you move from the home of one member to the home of another member in a designated sequence**

   Which correction should be made to sentence 9?

   (1) replace <u>a designated sequence</u> with <u>alphabetical order</u>
   (2) remove <u>of one member</u>
   (3) insert a question mark after <u>sequence</u>
   (4) insert a period after <u>sequence</u>
   (5) no correction is necessary

4. Sentence 14: **Focus on fiction, classics, self-help books, or some combination of genres?**

   Which correction should be made to sentence 14?

   (1) replace <u>?</u> with <u>!</u>
   (2) insert <u>The group wants to</u> before <u>Focus</u>
   (3) remove the comma after <u>fiction</u>
   (4) replace <u>?</u> with <u>.</u>
   (5) no correction is necessary

5. Sentence 18: **For instance, does the group want the host to use prepared questions to lead the discussion?**

   Which correction should be made to sentence 18?

   (1) replace <u>?</u> with <u>!</u>
   (2) remove <u>For instance,</u>
   (3) change <u>For instance</u> to <u>And</u>
   (4) replace <u>?</u> with <u>.</u>
   (5) no correction is necessary

Sentence Fragments

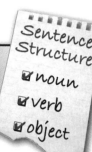

Sentence
Structure
☑ noun
☑ verb
☑ object

① Learn the Skill

A sentence that does not contain a subject, verb, or complete idea is called a **sentence fragment**. In many cases, a fragment is a clause or phrase that has become detached from the independent clause (main sentence): *But I said no.* In other cases, a fragment lacks a subject or a verb: *The warm afternoon sun.* To correct a fragment, you may attach it to the independent clause, or add a subject or a verb to the existing fragment.

② Practice the Skill

By mastering the skill of correcting sentence fragments, you will improve your writing and test-taking skills, especially as they relate to the GED Language Arts/Writing Test. Read the paragraph and strategies below. Then answer the question that follows.

Ⓐ Sentence 7 is a fragment because it begins with the conjunction *Although* and does not express a complete idea. A phrase that begins with a conjunction is called an introductory phrase or a dependent clause. This means that it must be connected to an independent clause in order to form a complete sentence.

Ⓑ To correct this fragment, connect the dependent clause to the independent clause: "this piece of advice would change my life in a positive way."

(A)
(1) "When you say no, mean it," Mrs. Morgan, my former U.S. History teacher, laughed, as she brushed a strand of reddish blond hair from her eyes. (2) We were standing together in the hallway outside one wing of my old school. (3) The warm afternoon sun kept us from other obligations. (4) "That's one thing that I always tried to do with my kids. (5) I didn't want to send the message that I didn't mean what I said. (6) If people think you don't mean what you say, they will take advantage of you," she finished, giving me a motherly look. **Ⓐ**(7) <u>Although I didn't know it at the time.</u> **Ⓑ**(8) <u>This piece of advice would change my life in a positive way</u>.

✓ TEST-TAKING TIPS

Memorize common conjunctions: *and, but, or, that, which, who, although,* and *because*. When you see a conjunction at the beginning of a sentence, examine the sentence carefully. You may be reading a fragment.

1. Sentences 7 and 8: **Although I didn't know it at the <u>time. This</u> piece of advice would change my life in a positive way.**

   Which is the best way to write the underlined portion of sentences 7 and 8? If the original is the best way, choose option (1).

   (1) time. This
   (2) time, this
   (3) time? This
   (4) time! This
   (5) time and this

UNIT 3

Directions: Choose the <u>one best answer</u> to each question.

<u>Questions 2 through 5</u> refer to the following information.

Help! I'm Sick

(A)

(1) There may not be a cure for the common cold. (2) But there are certainly strategies that one can utilize to alleviate some of the symptoms. (3) These symptoms may include runny nose, sinus congestion, and sneezing. (4) A sufferer may also experience a sore throat, cough, aching muscles, a headache, or a lack of appetite.

(B)

(5) A cold virus is likely to run its course in seven to ten days. (6) However, without some treatment. (7) It may be a miserable seven to ten days. (8) The two most beneficial tactics against a cold are rest and water. (9) Some cold medicines may also help make symptoms manageable. (10) What about the ancient remedy of chicken soup? (11) In fact, some research has shown that the heat, fluid, and salt may boost the immune system.

(C)

(12) The most effective strategy in battling a cold may be prevention. (13) If people limit their exposure to germs and boost their immune systems. (14) They may survive the cold season without carrying around a box of tissues. (15) People can limit their exposure to germs by washing their hands frequently, particularly after using the restroom or wiping a nose and before cooking food. (16) People can boost their immune systems by drinking water and eating yogurt. (17) They can also get plenty of sleep and take zinc supplements.

---

2. Sentences 1 and 2: **There may not be a cure for the common <u>cold. But</u> there are certainly strategies that one can utilize to alleviate some of the symptoms.**

   Which is the best way to write the underlined portion of sentences 1 and 2? If the original is the best way, choose option (1).

   (1) cold. But
   (2) cold, but
   (3) cold! But
   (4) cold? But
   (5) cold and

3. Sentences 6 and 7: **However, without some <u>treatment. It</u> may be a miserable seven to ten days.**

   Which is the best way to write the underlined portion of sentences 6 and 7? If the original is the best way, choose option (1).

   (1) treatment. It
   (2) treatment it
   (3) treatment? It
   (4) treatment, it
   (5) treatment and it

4. Sentences 13 and 14: **If people limit their exposure to germs and boost their immune <u>systems. They</u> may survive the cold season without carrying around a box of tissues.**

   Which is the best way to write the underlined portion of sentences 13 and 14? If the original is the best way, choose option (1).

   (1) systems. They
   (2) systems? They
   (3) system. They
   (4) systems! They
   (5) systems, they

Simple Sentences

Sentence
Structure
☑ noun
☑ verb
☑ object

① Learn the Skill

Now that you understand the difference between a complete sentence and a sentence fragment, you need to know that there are three types of complete sentences: simple, compound, and complex. A **simple sentence** contains a subject, a verb, and a single idea. Writers use simple sentences to emphasize important points.

② Practice the Skill

By mastering the skill of understanding simple sentences, you will improve your writing and test-taking skills, especially as they relate to the GED Language Arts/Writing Test. Read the paragraph and strategies below. Then answer the question that follows.

Ⓐ Sentence 10 is a simple sentence. It contains a subject that tells who or what the sentence is about and a verb that tells what the subject is doing or describes the subject's state of being. It also expresses a single idea.

Ⓑ A simple sentence may also contain other parts. For example, it may contain a transition (*Then*) and a direct object (*my mind*).

(C)
(1) Mrs. Morgan was right. (2) I needed to say no and mean it. (3) Uncle Joe wanted me to move to Little Rock. (4) He wanted me to work for him in his plumbing shop. (5) I had said "No" to his previous requests. (6) However, he kept pushing the issue. (7) I'm sure that he remembered another time. (8) I told him I didn't want to spend three weeks with him and Aunt Mary during my vacation. (9) I'd said "No" a dozen times in response to Uncle Joe's requests. **Ⓐ** (10) <u>Then, I changed my mind</u>. (11) He had no reason to think that this time would be any different.

☑ **TEST-TAKING TIPS**

To help you identify sentence types, circle or underline the subject, verb, and idea. If the sentence is simple, you will not find more than one subject, verb, or idea.

1. Sentence 10: **Then, <u>I changed</u> my mind.**

   The underlined portion of this simple sentence contains

   (1) a subject and a verb
   (2) a fragment and an object
   (3) an end mark
   (4) a transition and an object
   (5) an incomplete idea

Apply the Skill

Directions: Choose the <u>one best answer</u> to each question.

<u>Questions 2 through 4</u> refer to the following information.

What's Your Credit Score?

(A)

(1) If you've applied for a credit card or a bank loan recently, chances are good that information regarding your credit score factored into the result. (2) A credit score is a number between 300 and 850 that assesses the likelihood that you will pay back a creditor. (3) A low number is bad. (4) You are considered a credit risk. (5) You are not likely to pay your debts. (6) If your number is high, you are considered a good risk because you are likely to pay your debts.

(B)

(7) A credit score is based on one's credit history. (8) This history includes payment patterns, longevity, and current debt. (9) If your score is above 700, you are likely to get good lending rates. (10) If your score is below 600, you are likely to get high lending rates. (11) In fact, many creditors use 620 as the determining number for credit approval. (12) If your score is extremely low, you may be rejected for credit altogether.

(C)

(13) One's credit score is not a stable number. (14) It fluctuates. (15) It changes based on one's ongoing credit history. (16) Therefore, it is possible to raise a low credit score by adhering to the following tips. (17) Make sure that you pay your bills in a timely manner. (18) Also, do not maintain high balances on your credit cards. (19) Do not open credit accounts that you don't plan to use.

(20) To have a good credit score, you need to show that you are able to manage your credit. (21) Consequently, you need some credit cards and loans. (22) However, you must manage these accounts effectively. (23) Finally, you should know that a closed account doesn't disappear. (24) It may still affect your credit score.

---

2. Sentence 4: **You are considered a credit risk.**

   Which is the best way to describe sentence 4?

   (1) incomplete
   (2) an exclamation
   (3) a question
   (4) simple
   (5) a fragment

3. Sentence 8: **This history <u>includes</u> payment patterns, longevity, and current debt.**

   The underlined portion of this simple sentence contains

   (1) a verb
   (2) a subject
   (3) an incomplete idea
   (4) an end mark
   (5) a fragment

4. Sentence 14: **It fluctuates.**

   Which correction should be made to sentence 14?

   (1) insert an idea
   (2) remove sentence 14
   (3) insert a subject
   (4) insert a verb
   (5) no correction is necessary

Sentence
Structure
☑ noun
☑ verb
☑ object

Compound Sentences

① Learn the Skill

A **compound sentence** contains two independent clauses that are connected with a coordinating conjunction (*and, but, or*), semicolon (;), or conjunctive adverb (*finally, next, then*). You will learn more about adverbs later in this Unit. Remember that an independent clause can function alone as a complete but simple sentence. The structure of a compound sentence conveys a relationship between the ideas presented in the independent clauses, such as comparing and contrasting or cause and effect. The semicolon is a useful punctuation mark because it can be used between independent clauses that are not conjoined by *and*, *but*, or *or*; between independent clauses connected with *however, finally*, or *next*; and between a series that contains internal punctuation (such as this sentence).

② Practice the Skill

By mastering the skill of understanding compound sentences, you will improve your writing and test-taking skills, especially as they relate to the GED Language Arts/Writing Test. Read the paragraph and strategies below. Then answer the question that follows.

(A) Sentences 3 and 4 can be combined to form a compound sentence. If the two ideas show contrast, use *but* or *however* to form a compound sentence. If the ideas are closely related, use a semicolon.

(B) Sentence 6 is a compound sentence because it begins with the conjunctive adverb *However*. It also contains a semicolon and the coordinating conjunction *and*.

(C)

(1) Mrs. Morgan was right; I needed to say no and mean it. (2) Uncle Joe wanted me to move to Little Rock to work for him in his plumbing shop. **A** (3) <u>I had said "No" to his previous requests</u>. (4) <u>He kept pushing the issue</u>. (5) I'm sure he remembered the time I told him that I didn't want to spend three weeks with him and Aunt Mary during my vacation. **B** (6) <u>However</u>, I let my uncle talk me into making the visit<u>; and</u> I ended up having a great time. (7) I'd said "No" and then changed my mind a dozen times in response to Uncle Joe's requests. (8) He had no reason to think that this time would be any different.

✓ TEST-TAKING TIPS

To recognize a compound sentence, underline the two independent clauses, making sure that each clause has a subject, a verb, and an idea. Then circle the conjunction, adverb, or semicolon that connects the two clauses.

1. Sentences 3 and 4: **I had said "No" to his previous requests. He kept pushing the issue.**

    Which revision of sentences 3 and 4 forms a compound sentence?

    (1) Pushing the issue, I had said "No" to his previous requests.
    (2) I had said "No" to his previous issues.
    (3) I had said "No" to his previous requests, but he kept pushing the issue.
    (4) Previously requested, he kept pushing the issue.
    (5) He kept pushing the issue even though I said "No."

UNIT 3

③ Apply the Skill

Directions: Choose the <u>one best answer</u> to each question.

<u>Questions 2 through 4</u> refer to the following information.

Tigers

(A)

(1) Have you ever wondered how the tiger got its stripes? (2) In one ancient story, tiger was proud of its beautiful, golden coat. (3) However, tiger wasn't happy being beautiful. (4) He wanted to be smart, too. (5) He asked man for wisdom. (6) Man said that he would fetch wisdom from his house. (7) However, man said that he must first tie tiger to a tree so that tiger would not eat man's goats. (8) Tiger agreed. (9) Meanwhile, man and his goats sneaked away. (10) Later, tiger pulled himself free from the ropes, but the pulling caused black rope burns on tiger's skin. (11) Tiger did not get wisdom, and he lost his beauty.

(B)

(12) Perhaps the tiger's loss of beauty and his distrust of man led to a solitary life. (13) The tiger has no friends. (14) It lives alone and hunts at night in the regions of Asia and Russia. (15) It eats deer, pigs, buffalo, and antelope. (16) The tiger uses its 200 to 500 pounds of body weight to knock down its prey, killing the victim with a lethal bite to the neck.

(C)

(17) The story regarding the tiger's stripes reveals the tiger's lone enemy: man. (18) People hunt tigers for their fur and body parts. (19) People also kill tigers to protect communities, and people overtake tiger habitats to build cities.

(D)

(20) Many years ago, there were tens of thousands of tigers in the world. (21) Today, there are only about five to seven thousand. (22) Several types of tigers, including the Caspian, Javan, and Bali, are already extinct. (23) Six other types, including the Bengal and Siberian, are endangered. (24) Interestingly, man holds the wisdom the tiger wants in the story; however, man has not used this wisdom to prevent the extinction of this magnificent (and beautiful) beast.

---

2. Sentences 3 and 4: **However, tiger wasn't happy being beautiful. He wanted to be smart, too.**

   Which revision of sentences 3 and 4 forms a compound sentence?

   (1) Because tiger wanted to be smart, he wasn't happy being beautiful.
   (2) However, tiger wasn't happy being beautiful; he wanted to be smart, too.
   (3) Tiger wanted to be beautiful and smart.
   (4) Tiger was smart enough to understand the insignificance of beauty.
   (5) Tiger wasn't happy because he wanted to be smart too.

3. Sentence 19: **People also kill tigers to protect communities, and people overtake tiger habitats to build cities.**

   Which strategy did the writer use to form this compound sentence?

   (1) a conjunctive adverb
   (2) a semicolon
   (3) simple sentences
   (4) a coordinating conjunction
   (5) fragments

4. Which of the following sentences is a compound sentence?

   (1) Interestingly, man holds the wisdom the tiger wants in the story; however, man has not used this wisdom to prevent the extinction of this magnificent (and beautiful) beast.
   (2) During the 1900s, there were about 100,000 tigers in the world.
   (3) Six other types, including the Bengal and Siberian, are endangered.
   (4) Today, there are only about three to four thousand.
   (5) Several types of tigers, including the Caspian, Javan, and Bali, are already extinct.

Complex Sentences

Sentence
Structure
☑ noun
☑ verb
☑ object

① Learn the Skill

A **complex sentence** contains an independent clause and a dependent clause. An independent clause can stand alone as a sentence, but a dependent clause is a sentence fragment unless it is attached to an independent clause. The function of a dependent clause is to add information to an independent clause. Words such as *although* or *because* are used to introduce a dependent clause.

② Practice the Skill

By mastering the skill of understanding complex sentences, you will improve your writing and test-taking skills, especially as they relate to the GED Language Arts/Writing Test. Read the paragraph and strategies below. Then answer the question that follows.

A Sentence 1 begins with the word *although*— a subordinating conjunction—which means that the sentence is a dependent clause. Because this sentence does not express a complete idea, it is a fragment and cannot stand alone.

B To correct this fragment, connect it to the independent clause that follows: "It was valuable."

(E)
A (1) Although Mrs. Morgan's advice was simple. **B** (2) It was valuable. (3) She taught me the importance of matching my words with my thoughts. (4) By following this advice, I gained self-confidence. (5) Any expert in psychology will agree that self-confidence is an important aspect of one's self-esteem. (6) Now, I control my own future by choosing my words carefully. (7) I say what I mean, and I get what I want.

TEST-TAKING TIPS

To identify complex sentences, memorize common subordinating conjunctions such as *after, although, as, because, before, if, in order to, unless, when, where, whether,* and *while.* These words are clues that you're reading a complex sentence.

1. Sentences 1 and 2: **Although Mrs. Morgan's advice was <u>simple. It</u> was valuable**

   Which is the best way to write the underlined portion of sentences 1 and 2? If the original is the best way, choose option (1).

   (1) simple. It
   (2) simple, it
   (3) simple; it
   (4) simple! It
   (5) simple? It

Directions: Choose the <u>one best answer</u> to each question.

<u>Questions 2 through 4</u> refer to the following information.

Paper Mache

(A)

(1) Gift giving can put a burden on anyone's budget. (2) Before you fight the crowds at the local mall and max out your credit cards, you should try making your own gifts. (3) You'll find this activity enjoyable and cheap. (4) One easy technique for making homemade gifts is paper mache. (5) You may not have engaged in this craft since grade school, but it's time to revisit it.

(B)

(6) You probably have a majority of the needed supplies in your home right now. (7) You need many small, torn pieces of paper. (8) You can use newspaper, but it may have to be painted later. (9) A good alternative to newspaper is colored tissue paper. (10) You should also consider using words printed in decorative font on torn pieces of paper. (11) You will also need a form. (12) You can use pre-existing forms such as small, sturdy boxes, which make great jewelry cases. (13) You can also create your own forms by using cardboard or balloons and masking tape. (14) Finally, you need a paste. (15) While it's possible to make your own paste with water and flour, why bother with the mess? (16) It's simpler and cleaner to mix glue and water or to use wallpaper paste.

(C)

(17) When you have your supplies, the fun begins. (18) Simply dip each small piece of paper in the paste mixture and place it on your form. (19) Continue this process by layering and smoothing the edges of the small pieces of paper over one another to create a mosaic effect. (20) If you're using colored tissue paper for this step. (21) You'll notice that the layering creates additional colors. (22) Make sure to cover every inch of space on the form. (23) When the coverage is complete, leave the form to dry for several hours. (24) After the form is dry, you can decorate it with paint, glitter, ribbons, or other accessories as desired. (25) These gifts may be too pretty to wrap. (26) Just add a bow and a gift tag and distribute.

---

2. Which of the following sentences is a complex sentence?

   (1) One easy technique for making homemade gifts is paper mache.
   (2) Gift giving can put a burden on anyone's budget.
   (3) You may not have engaged in this craft since grade school, but it's time to revisit it.
   (4) Before you fight the crowds at the local mall and max out your credit cards, you should try making your own gifts.
   (5) You'll find this activity enjoyable and cheap.

3. Sentence 15: **While it's possible to make your own paste with water and flour, why bother with the mess?**

Which word in sentence 15 is a subordinating conjunction?

   (1) possible
   (2) while
   (3) make
   (4) bother
   (5) paste

4. Sentences 20 and 21: **If you're using colored tissue paper for this <u>step. You'll</u> notice that the layering creates additional colors.**

Which is the best way to write the underlined portion of sentences 20 and 21? If the original is the best way, choose option (1).

   (1) step. You'll
   (2) step: You'll
   (3) step, you'll
   (4) step. You will
   (5) step; you will

Combining Sentences

Sentence Structure
☑ noun
☑ verb
☑ object

① Learn the Skill

Now that you understand the structure of simple, compound, and complex sentences, you can focus your attention on the effect these sentence types have on writing. Sometimes writing too many simple sentences in a row can be repetitive. In this case, you should combine the shorter sentences into one compound or complex sentence. This method is called **combining sentences**. For example: *I bought a dog. I bought a leash. I bought some dog food.* These three sentences would be more effective if combined into one sentence: *I bought a dog, a leash, and some dog food.*

② Practice the Skill

By mastering the skill of combining sentences, you will improve your writing and test-taking skills, especially as they relate to the GED Language Arts/Writing Test. Read the paragraph and strategies below. Then answer the question that follows.

A Read sentences 7, 8, and 9. Notice that the repetition of the word *time* makes these sentences choppy and repetitious.

B Sentences 7, 8, and 9 can be combined: *I'm sure Uncle Joe remembered the time when I told him I didn't want to spend three weeks with him and Aunt Mary during my summer vacation.* Add or delete words as necessary, as long as the new sentence retains the meaning of the original sentence.

(C)

(1) Mrs. Morgan was right. (2) I needed to say no and mean it. (3) Uncle Joe wanted me to move to Little Rock. (4) He wanted me to work for him in his plumbing shop. (5) I had said "No" to his previous requests. (6) However, he kept pushing the issue. (7) <u>I'm sure that Uncle Joe remembered another time</u>. (8) <u>The time was when I told him I didn't want to spend three weeks with him and Aunt Mary</u>. (9) <u>The time was during my vacation</u>. (10) I'd said "No" a dozen times in response to Uncle Joe's requests. (11) Then, I changed my mind. (12) He had no reason to think that this time would be any different.

✏ WRITING STRATEGIES

When combining sentences, use *and, but, or, however, finally,* or semicolons to form compound sentences. Use *although* and *because* to form complex sentences. You can also add phrases to connect ideas, eliminate repeated words, and/or use commas to create a series: *red, white, and blue.*

1. Sentences 3 and 4: **Uncle Joe wanted me to move to Little Rock. He wanted me to work for him in his plumbing shop.**

   Which of the following is the most effective revision of sentences 3 and 4?

   (1) Uncle Joe wanted me to be a plumber in Little Rock.
   (2) As a plumber, Uncle Joe wanted me to move to Little Rock to work.
   (3) Uncle Joe wanted me to move to Little Rock and work for him in his plumbing shop.
   (4) He wanted me to work for him in Little Rock in his plumbing shop.
   (5) Uncle Joe is a plumber in Little Rock who wanted me to work with him.

UNIT 3

Apply the Skill

Directions: Choose the <u>one best answer</u> to each question.

<u>Questions 2 and 3</u> refer to the following information.

Notice for Emergency Awareness

(A)

(1) A good home is a safe home. (2) A safe home is a place where all family members know what to do in the event of an emergency. (3) An emergency may include a fire. (4) An emergency may include an earthquake. (5) An emergency may include a hurricane or a tornado. (6) It is a good idea to create a family safety plan. (7) To create a family safety plan, follow these tips.

(B)

1. (8) Establish an escape route from each room of your home. (9) Every member of the family should know how to get out of the home without assistance.

(C)

2. (10) Select meeting locations in case family members become separated. (11) One location should be in your neighborhood while another should be elsewhere.

(D)

3. (12) Select a person outside the city to contact in the event of an emergency. (13) Make sure that every family member has the cell or telephone number and e-mail address of this person.

(E)

4. (14) Prepare an emergency card for each family member to carry with him or her. (15) The card should contain emergency contact information, medical conditions and medications, and the names of family members.

(F)

5. (16) Place a note on a calendar reminding the family to review the emergency plan two times per year. (17) The family should also practice escaping from the home during each review.

---

2. Sentences 1 and 2: **A good home is a safe home. A safe home is a place where all family members know what to do in the event of an emergency.**

Which of the following is the most effective revision of sentences 1 and 2?

(1) A good, safe home is a place where family members know what to do.
(2) A safe home is a place that is good.
(3) A good home is a safe home, and a safe home is a place where all family members know what to do in the event of an emergency.
(4) Family members know what to do in an emergency if they live in a good home.
(5) Family members in a safe home make up a good home where they know what to do in an emergency.

3. Sentences 3, 4, and 5: **An emergency may include a fire. An emergency may include an earthquake. An emergency may include a hurricane or a tornado.**

Which of the following is the most effective revision of sentences 3, 4, and 5?

(1) An emergency may include a fire, earthquake, hurricane, or tornado.
(2) Fires and earthquakes are emergencies. Hurricanes and tornados are emergencies.
(3) In the event of an emergency, such as a hurricane or tornado, check for fires and earthquakes.
(4) Fires and earthquakes are more serious emergencies than hurricanes or tornadoes.
(5) Emergencies may include natural disasters.

Run-On Sentences

Sentence
Structure
☑ noun
☑ verb
☑ object

① Learn the Skill

Conjunctions, commas, and semicolons are important when combining sentences or writing compound sentences. When you combine two or more independent clauses incorrectly, the result is a **run-on sentence**: *She gave me advice it was good.* When you use a comma to form a compound sentence, you must make sure to include a coordinating conjunction. If the conjunction is missing, you have created a **comma splice** that must be corrected. To repair a comma splice, use a period to form two sentences or add a coordinating conjunction, such as *and*, *but*, or *or*.

② Practice the Skill

By mastering the skill of correcting run-on sentences, you will improve your writing and test-taking skills, especially as they relate to the GED Language Arts/Writing Test. Read the paragraph and strategies below. Then answer the question that follows.

A Sentence 2 contains two independent clauses that are combined with a comma, creating a comma splice.

B To correct sentence 2, place a period after *school*, followed by a new sentence. It should now read: *We were standing together in the hallway outside one wing of my old school. The warm afternoon sun kept us from other obligations.*

(A)

(1) "When you say no, mean it," Mrs. Morgan, my former U.S. History teacher, laughed as she brushed a strand of reddish, blond hair from her eyes. (2) <u>We were standing together in the hallway outside one wing of my old school, the warm afternoon sun kept us from other obligations</u>. (3) "That's one thing I always tried to do with my kids. (4) I didn't want to send the message that I didn't mean what I said. (5) If people think you don't mean what you say, they will take advantage of you," she finished, giving me a motherly look. (6) I didn't know it at the time, this piece of advice would change my life in a positive way.

☑ TEST-TAKING TIPS

To identify a run-on sentence, underline the independent clauses in a long sentence. Then, determine whether the clauses are combined correctly using commas, semicolons, and/or conjunctions.

1. Sentence 6: **I didn't know it at the time, this piece of advice would change my life in a positive way.**

   Which correction should be made to sentence 6?

   (1) replace <u>this</u> with <u>but</u>
   (2) insert <u>but</u> before <u>this</u>
   (3) remove the comma after <u>time</u>
   (4) insert a semicolon after <u>life</u>
   (5) no correction is necessary

Directions: Choose the <u>one best answer</u> to each question.

<u>Questions 2 through 4</u> refer to the following information.

**Employee Manual
Work-Related Injuries**

Minor Injuries

(A)

1. (1) Do not delay, report all minor injuries to the department manager and the Human Resources Department.

2. (2) The Human Resources Department is responsible for the following actions: reporting the claim to the insurance company, referring the employee to an appropriate healthcare provider, and working with a department manager to secure any needed recovery time.

3. (3) Employees receive permission from the healthcare provider they will resume work-related duties.

Major Injuries

(B)

1. (4) Without delay, place calls to 911 and the Security Department.

2. (5) The Security Department will contact the Human Resources Department they will also provide a copy of the injury report.

3. (6) Seek immediate medical treatment at the nearest emergency facility.

4. (7) As soon as is possible, contact the Human Resources Department to complete an incident report and receive further counseling.

---

2. Sentence 1: **Do not delay, report all minor injuries to the department manager and the Human Resources Department.**

   Which correction should be made to sentence 1?

   (1) remove the comma after <u>delay</u>
   (2) change <u>and</u> to <u>, but</u>
   (3) insert a semicolon after <u>delay</u>
   (4) insert <u>but</u> before <u>report</u>
   (5) no correction is necessary

3. Sentence 3: <u>**Employees receive permission from the healthcare provider they**</u> **will resume work-related duties.**

   Which is the best way to write the underlined portion of sentence 3? If the original is the best way, choose option (1).

   (1) Employees receive permission from the healthcare provider they
   (2) After employees receive permission from the healthcare provider; moreover they
   (3) Employees receive permission from the healthcare provider, or they
   (4) Employees receive permission from the healthcare provider, they
   (5) When employees receive permission from the healthcare provider, they

4. Sentence 5: **The Security Department will contact the Human Resources Department they will also provide a copy of the injury report.**

   Which correction should be made to sentence 5?

   (1) insert <u>, and</u> after <u>Human Resources Department</u>
   (2) replace <u>also</u> with <u>too</u>
   (3) replace <u>.</u> with <u>?</u>
   (4) insert <u>In order that</u> before <u>The Security Department</u>
   (5) no correction is necessary

Misplaced Modifiers

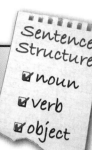

① Learn the Skill

Modifiers, such as adjectives, adverbs, and phrases, tell more information about another part of a sentence, such as subjects, verbs, and nouns. A **misplaced modifier** misleads readers by seeming to describe the wrong item and results in a sentence being difficult to read: *The food was in the bowl that the dog ate.* To correct a misplaced modifier, move the modifier or modifying phrase, *that the dog ate,* closer to the word or phrase it is meant to describe: *The food that the dog ate was in the bowl.*

② Practice the Skill

By mastering the skill of correcting misplaced modifiers, you will improve your writing and test-taking skills, especially as they relate to the GED Language Arts/Writing Test. Read the paragraph and strategies below. Then answer the question that follows.

A Which idea does the writer intend the adverb *carefully* to modify? *Control my future* or *choose my words?*

B If the writer means that he controls his words carefully, the modifier can be moved before the action it modifies: *choosing.* If the writer means that he controls his future carefully, then the writer might create an introductory phrase: *By choosing my words, I carefully control my future.*

(E)
(1) Although Mrs. Morgan's advice was simple, it was valuable. (2) She taught me the importance of matching my words with my thoughts. (3) By following this advice, I gained self-confidence. (4) Now, I control my own future <u>carefully</u> by choosing my words. (5) I say what I mean, and I get what I want.

☑ TEST-TAKING TIPS

Misplaced modifiers are difficult to identify when reading quickly. Underline descriptive words and phrases. Then slow the pace of your reading, and think about the meaning the writer intends. If the meaning is unclear, you may have found a misplaced modifier.

1. Sentence 4: **Now, I control my own future carefully by choosing my words.**

   Which correction should be made to sentence 4?

   (1) move <u>carefully</u> to before <u>choosing</u>
   (2) move <u>carefully</u> to before <u>control</u>
   (3) move <u>carefully</u> to follow <u>choosing</u>
   (4) move <u>carefully</u> to follow <u>control</u>
   (5) no correction is necessary

Directions: Choose the one best answer to each question.

Questions 2 through 4 refer to the following information.

Potluck Party

(A)

(1) For your next family gathering or party, consider putting a south-of-the-border spin on the traditional potluck by hosting a taco bar. (2) It's fun and inexpensive. (3) Additionally, the menu also assures you of a decorating theme.

(B)

(4) You provide the menu basics: an appetizer of fried or baked tortilla chips and an array of salsas; hard and soft taco shells; and a meat filling such as ground beef or chicken or both. (5) You are also responsible for the decorations and entertainment. (6) In the background, consider using cactuses as centerpieces and playing Salsa music.

(C)

(7) Instruct your guests to bring toppings for the tacos, which are spicy. (8) You can suggest these traditional items: cheese, lettuce, tomatoes, sour cream, and guacamole. (9) However, you should also encourage your guests to exercise a little creativity when they plan their offerings. (10) They may bring corn, black beans, Spanish rice, grilled vegetables, green chili or tomatillo salsas, and so on.

(D)

(11) Arrange a buffet table by placing the hard and soft taco shells and the meat fillings at the end of the table where the serving line will begin. (12) Then, place the toppings and sauces to follow. (13) Encourage your guests to build their tacos as they experiment with unusual flavor combinations systematically.

---

2. Sentence 6: **In the background, consider using cactuses as centerpieces and playing Salsa music.**

   Which correction should be made to sentence 6?

   (1) remove the comma after background
   (2) move Salsa to follow music
   (3) move in the background to follow music
   (4) insert the host should before consider
   (5) no correction is necessary

3. Sentence 7: **Instruct your guests to bring toppings for the tacos, which are spicy.**

   Which correction should be made to sentence 7?

   (1) move spicy to before toppings and remove , which are
   (2) remove , which are spicy
   (3) move spicy to before tacos and remove , which are
   (4) insert a comma after guests
   (5) no correction is necessary

4. Sentence 13: **Encourage your guests to build their tacos as they experiment with unusual flavor combinations systematically.**

   Which correction should be made to sentence 13?

   (1) move systematically to before combinations
   (2) remove unusual
   (3) insert a comma after combinations
   (4) move systematically to follow tacos
   (5) no correction is necessary

Sentence
Structure
☑ noun
☑ verb
☑ object

Dangling Modifiers

① Learn the Skill

Remember that modifiers, such as adjectives, adverbs, and phrases, tell more information about subjects, verbs, and nouns. A **dangling modifier** describes an unnamed subject: *Having bought a new dog, the leash was purchased.* To correct a dangling modifier, add the subject meant to be described by the sentence. To do this, create a dependent clause or replace the subject of the independent clause: *Having bought a new dog, Jane purchased a leash.*

② Practice the Skill

By mastering the skill of correcting dangling modifiers, you will improve your writing and test-taking skills, especially as they relate to the GED Language Arts/Writing Test. Read the paragraph and strategies below. Then answer the question that follows.

A The subject of the modifier in sentence 3, "By following this advice," must be stated in the independent clause that follows the modifier. In this case, the subject is *self-confidence*. Does the writer mean that *self-confidence* followed Mrs. Morgan's advice? No, the writer means that *he* followed the advice.

B Sometimes in order to correct a dangling modifier, the words in the clauses must be rearranged. To correct sentence 3, replace the incorrect subject, *self-confidence*, with the correct subject: *By following this advice, I achieved self-confidence.*

(E)
(1) Although Mrs. Morgan's advice was simple, value was found. (2) She taught me the importance of matching my words with my thoughts. (3) <u>By following this advice, self-confidence was achieved</u>. (4) Any expert in psychology will agree that self-confidence is an important aspect of one's self-esteem. (5) Now, I control my own future by choosing my words carefully. (6) I say what I mean, and I get what I want.

✓ **TEST-TAKING TIPS**

Dangling modifiers tend to appear at the beginning of sentences. Additionally, dangling modifiers often contain *–ing* words or *to+verb* phrases. When reading multipart sentences, make sure that the correct subject follows introductory phrases or clauses.

1. Sentence 1: **Although Mrs. Morgan's advice was simple, value was found.**

   Which is the most effective revision of sentence 1?

   (1) Value was found from the simple advice.
   (2) Although Mrs. Morgan's advice was simple, it was valuable.
   (3) Value, from Mrs. Morgan's simple advice, was found.
   (4) This advice, by following value, was simple.
   (5) Although Mrs. Morgan's simple advice was found to be valuable.

UNIT 3

Directions: Choose the one best answer to each question.

Questions 2 through 4 refer to the following memorandum.

> **Riddle Retailer**
> Human Resources Department
> Corporate Headquarters
> 361 First Street
> Bentonville, AR 27513
>
> **To:** All Employees of Riddle Retailers
> **From:** Alice Underwood, Director of Human Resources
> **Subject:** Fitness Fee
>
> **(A)**
> (1) Beginning with the next calendar year, Riddle Retailers will collect an additional $30.00 per month health insurance fee from employees who are overweight or who smoke. (2) Visiting with physicians, physicals must be obtained. (3) Any employee whose doctor identifies problems with weight, lung health, blood pressure, or cholesterol levels will be monitored by his or her physician to seek improvement in these areas. (4) To ensure success, employer-sponsored wellness programs will be available. (5) Fees will be charged to any employee who does not show monthly gains in problem areas over the course of the year.
>
> **(B)**
> (6) The requisite paperwork for this program will follow this memo. (7) Having until the end of this calendar year, paperwork and physicals must be completed. (8) If you have any questions, please see your department supervisor.

2. Sentence 2: **Visiting with physicians, physicals must be obtained.**

   Which is the most effective revision of sentence 2?

   (1) Physicals must be obtained by visiting with physicians.
   (2) Physicals, from physicians, must be obtained.
   (3) From physicians, employees must obtain physicals.
   (4) Physicians must visit and obtain physicals.
   (5) no revision is necessary

3. Sentence 4: **To ensure success, employer-sponsored wellness programs will be available.**

   Which is the most effective revision of sentence 4?

   (1) To ensure success, employees will be eligible for employer-sponsored wellness programs.
   (2) Employer-sponsored wellness programs, to ensure success, will be available.
   (3) Employer-sponsored wellness programs will be available to ensure success.
   (4) Available to ensure success are employer-sponsored wellness programs.
   (5) no revision is necessary

4. Sentence 7: **Having until the end of this calendar year, paperwork and physicals must be completed.**

   Which subject is missing from the independent clause in sentence 7?

   (1) employers
   (2) physicians
   (3) retailers
   (4) employees
   (5) no subject is missing

Parallel Structure

① Learn the Skill

As a writer, you must determine the importance of the ideas you present. If ideas are of equal importance, you are likely to use compound sentences or a series of words or phrases. To support the message that all ideas in a sentence are equally important, writers present the ideas using the same word form or sentence structure: *I like running, ~~to swim~~ swimming, and biking.* This technique is called **parallel structure**.

② Practice the Skill

By mastering the skill of using parallel structure, you will improve your writing and test-taking skills, especially as they relate to the GED Language Arts/Writing Test. Read the paragraph and strategies below. Then answer the question that follows.

A In sentence 6, the writer presents two ideas. He says what he means, and he gets what he wants. These ideas are dependent upon one another and therefore equally important.

(E)
(1) Although Mrs. Morgan's advice was simple, it was valuable. (2) She taught me the importance of matching my words with my thoughts. (3) By following this advice, I achieved self-confidence, standing up for myself. (4) Any expert in psychology will agree that self-confidence is an important aspect of one's self-esteem. (5) Now, I control my own future by choosing my words carefully. **A**(6) I say what I mean, getting what I want.

B However, the writer does not maintain parallel structure when presenting these two equally important ideas. The writer begins with the *subject+verb* combination *I say.* Then shifts to the *–ing* form of the verb *get* and eliminates the subject *I.* The corrected sentence should read *I say what I mean, and I get what I want.*

☑ **TEST-TAKING TIPS**

The use of *and, but,* or *or* to connect items in a series or to form a compound sentence should alert you to examine a sentence for parallel structure. Carefully examine each answer option before selecting your final answer.

1. Sentence 3: **By following this advice, I achieved self-confidence, standing up for myself.**

   Which correction should be made to sentence 3?

   (1) replace <u>achieved</u> with <u>achieve</u>
   (2) move <u>standing up for myself</u> before <u>I achieved</u>
   (3) change <u>standing</u> to <u>and I stood</u>
   (4) insert a semicolon after <u>self-confidence</u>
   (5) no correction is necessary

Directions: Choose the <u>one best answer</u> to each question.

Questions 2 through 4 refer to the following information.

**Notice for Career Development Opportunity
How to Be a More Persuasive Speaker**

(A)

(1) Join your colleagues for an afternoon of fellowship and career development. (2) World-renowned expert in communication skills, Julie Taylor will be on site giving instruction and to enlighten participants in the fine art of persuasive speaking. (3) Ms. Taylor will address the following persuasive speaking strategies:

(B)

• (4) **Offer Less Than You're Willing to Give**

(5) This strategy creates room for bargaining and negotiations. (6) A second party will feel satisfied when he or she persuades you to offer a little more.

• (7) **Point out Similarities**

(8) This strategy creates the impression that two parties are "on the same page." (9) When similarities seem to outweigh differences, people are more likely to compromise.

• (10) **Use Someone Else's Language to State Your Idea**

(11) This strategy creates the impression that you agree with a second party. (12) People like to hear themselves talk. (13) Use this human trait to frame your message.

• (14) **Personalizing or Making Human Your Message**

(15) This strategy creates an emotional connection to abstract ideas or facts.

---

2. Sentence 2: **World-renowned expert in communication skills, Julie Taylor will be on site <u>giving instruction</u> and to enlighten participants in the fine art of persuasive speaking.**

Which is the best way to write the underlined portion of sentence 2? If the original is the best way, choose option (1).

(1) giving instruction
(2) gave instruction
(3) to give instruction
(4) given instruction
(5) instruction given

3. Sentence 5: **This strategy creates room for bargaining and negotiations.**

Which is the most effective revision of sentence 5?

(1) This strategy creates room for bargaining and negotiating.
(2) Bargaining and negotiations are the result of this strategy.
(3) This strategy, creating room for bargaining and negotiating.
(4) Creating room for bargaining and strategy, negotiations follow.
(5) no revision is necessary

4. Sentence 14: **Personalizing or Making Human Your Message**

Which is the most effective revision of sentence 14?

(1) Humanize or Personalizing Your Message
(2) Personalizing (or Making Human) Your Message
(3) Personing or Humaning Your Message
(4) Personalize or Humanize Your Message
(5) no revision is necessary

The Unit Review is structured to resemble the GED Language Arts/Writing Test. Be sure to read each question and all possible answers very carefully before choosing your answer.

To record your answers, fill in the numbered circle that corresponds to the answer you select for each question in the Unit Review.

Do not rest your pencil on the answer area while considering your answer. Make no stray or unnecessary marks. If you change an answer, erase your first mark completely.

Mark only one answer space for each question; multiple answers will be scored as incorrect.

Sample Question

Sentence 3: **The backup power will serve a health care facility.**

Which kind of sentence is sentence 3?

(1) complex
(2) fragment
(3) simple
(4) combination
(5) compound

①②●④⑤

Directions: Choose the <u>one best answer</u> to each question.

<u>Questions 1 through 5</u> refer to the following information.

Request for Proposal

Project Overview

(A)

(1) The project involves installing two emergency power generator sets. (2) The power generator sets will provide back-up power. (3) The backup power will serve a health care facility. (4) The generator sets provide emergency power to administrative offices, facility support buildings, and resident quarters. (5) The generator sets are replacement sets. (6) These replacement sets are being installed to serve additional loading. (7) The additional loading has been or is being connected to the system. (8) In the same location where the existing service pads are located. (9) Two replacement foundations will need to be installed. (10) To ascertain the current stability conditions and existing concrete depth, core soil samples are needed. (11) To explain the condition and stability of the existing soil and any corrections that will need to be made to accommodate the anticipated foundation loading. (12) A report shall be developed.

Scope of Work

(B)

(13) The scope of work for this project shall include but not necessarily be limited to:

- site visitations
- soil samples and testing
- drilling and repair of concrete
- preparation and transmittal of reports
- recommendations for surface support

UNIT 3

1. Sentences 1, 2, and 3: **The project involves installing two emergency power generator sets. The power generator sets will provide back-up power. The backup power will serve a health care facility.**

   Which of the following is the most effective revision of sentences 1, 2, and 3?

   (1) Because the health care facility requires back-up power, the project involves installing two emergency power generator sets.
   (2) The project, which will provide back-up power for a health care facility.
   (3) The health care facility that requires back-up power needs the project to install two emergency power generator sets.
   (4) The project on the health care facility needs back-up power.
   (5) The health care facility hopes the installation of two emergency generator sets will provide back-up power by the project. ①②③④⑤

2. Sentences 5, 6, and 7: **The generator sets are replacement sets. These replacement sets are being installed to serve additional loading. The additional loading has been or is being connected to the system.**

   Which of the following is the most effective revision of sentences 5, 6, and 7?

   (1) Generator sets, which are replacement sets, are being installed to serve additional loading.
   (2) Additional loading, will be served by installing generator sets that are replacements.
   (3) Replacement generator sets are being installed to serve the additional loading, which has been or is being connected to the system.
   (4) Generator sets that are replacement sets will serve additional connections that have been or are being loaded to the system.
   (5) Loading replacement generator sets will connect additional installations to the system. ①②③④⑤

3. Sentences 8 and 9: **In the same location where the existing service pads are <u>located. Two</u> replacement foundations will need to be installed.**

   Which correction should be made to the underlined portion of sentences 8 and 9? If the original is the best way, choose option (1).

   (1) located. Two
   (2) located, two
   (3) located. Consequently, two
   (4) located, but two
   (5) located. Nonetheless, two
   ①②③④⑤

4. Sentences 11 and 12: **To explain the condition and stability of the existing soil and any corrections that will need to be made to accommodate the anticipated foundation <u>loading. A</u> report shall be developed.**

   Which correction should be made to the underlined portion of sentences 11 and 12? If the original is the best way, choose option (1).

   (1) loading. A
   (2) loading: a
   (3) loading; a
   (4) loading? A
   (5) loading, a
   ①②③④⑤

5. Sentence 13: **The scope of work for this project shall include but not necessarily be limited to:**

   Which correction should be made to sentence 13 to make it complete?

   (1) replace <u>to</u> with <u>too</u>
   (2) insert <u>the following items</u> after <u>limited to</u>
   (3) remove the colon
   (4) change <u>shall</u> to <u>will</u>
   (5) no correction is necessary
   ①②③④⑤

Directions: Choose the <u>one best answer</u> to each question.

<u>Questions 6 through 9</u> refer to the following memorandum.

Johnson Engineering
Office Management
Corporate Headquarters
628 Ferncreek Blvd.
Volcano, AR 11223

To: All Employees
From: Tonya Smith
Subject: Correspondence

Date: November 29, 2009

(A)

(1) As business activity increases. (2) We need to remind all employees of the procedure for sending correspondence. (3) All correspondence requires a letter of transmittal. (4) Whether it is delivered electronically or via hard copy.

(B)

(5) The letter of transmittal contains the following information: company contact information, a description of the attached documents, and an explanation of what we expect the recipient to do with the attached documents. (6) Additionally, you may include remarks. (7) You may also include sources as necessary.

(C)

(8) Each letter of transmittal must also be signed by the appropriate supervisor copies of each letter of transmittal should be filed in the appropriate project folder.

(D)

(9) Copies of the company letter of transmittal are available in hard copy through the manager of each department. (10) Copies of the company letter of transmittal are available electronically through the manager of each department.

---

6. Sentences 1 and 2: **As business activity <u>increases. We</u> need to remind all employees of the procedure for sending correspondence.**

Which is the best way to write the underlined portion of sentences 1 and 2? If the original is the best way, choose option (1).

(1) increases. We
(2) increases, we
(3) increases; we
(4) increases, and
(5) increases? We

①②③④⑤

7. Sentences 3 and 4: **All correspondence requires a letter of transmittal. Whether it is delivered electronically or via hard copy.**

Which of the following is the most effective revision of sentences 3 and 4?

(1) All correspondence, whether it is delivered electronically or via hard copy, requires a letter of transmittal.
(2) Whether it's delivered electronically or via hard copy. It requires a letter of transmittal.
(3) All correspondence requires a letter of transmittal. It is delivered electronically or via hard copy.
(4) A letter of transmittal, both via hard copy or electronically, is required.
(5) All correspondence requires a letter of transmittal. However, it is delivered via hard copy or electronically.

①②③④⑤

8. Sentence 8: **Each letter of transmittal must also be signed by the appropriate supervisor copies of each letter of transmittal should be filed in the appropriate project folder.**

What type of sentence is sentence 8?

(1) complete
(2) run-on
(3) compound
(4) complex
(5) fragment

①②③④⑤

9. Sentence 9 and 10: **Copies of the company letter of transmittal are available in hard copy through the manager of each department. Copies of the company letter of transmittal are available electronically through the manager of each department.**

Which of the following is the most effective revision of sentences 9 and 10?

(1) Copies of the company letter of transmittal are available from your manager.
(2) Copies of the company letter of transmittal are available in hard copy or electronically.
(3) Copies of the company letter of transmittal are available in hard copy and electronically through the manager of each department.
(4) Your manager will provide you with a copy of the company letter of transmittal.
(5) Hard copies of the company letter of transmittal are available; electronic copies too.

①②③④⑤

Directions: Choose the <u>one best answer</u> to each question.

<u>Questions 10 through 15</u> refer to the following information.

Heart Disease and Diet

(A)

(1) Heart disease is a serious problem in the United States. (2) Heart disease occurs as the result of fatty plaque deposits in the arteries that deliver blood to the heart. (3) These plaque deposits cause narrowing and hard arteries. (4) This condition does not allowing the heart to receive the blood it needs for healthy functioning. (5) However, there is good news for American men and women. (6) Avoiding the complications that come with heart disease such as chest pain, stroke, or heart attack, a healthy heart is possible through diet.

(B)

(7) There are several foods that you should eat to keep your heart healthy. (8) These foods include fruits, vegetables, grains, low-fat dairy products, fish, chicken, turkey, beans, eggs, and nuts. (9) You should only eat the so-called "good" fats, polyunsaturated and monounsaturated. (10) These fats occur in vegetable oils, fish, and nuts.

(C)

(11) There are several foods that you should limit or avoid to keep your heart healthy. (12) These foods include salt, sugar, processed foods that contain trans fat, and cholesterol found in some meats and fatty dairy products. (13) You should also avoid the so-called "bad" fat. (14) Saturated fat is found in some meats and fatty dairy products.

---

10. Sentence 1: **Heart disease is a serious problem in the United States.**

What kind of sentence is sentence 1?

(1) complex
(2) compound
(3) fragment
(4) simple
(5) combined

① ② ③ ④ ⑤

11. Sentence 3: **These plaque deposits cause narrowing and hard arteries.**

Which is the best way to write the underlined portion of sentence 3? If the original is the best way, choose option (1).

(1) narrowing and hard arteries
(2) narrowing and hardening arteries
(3) narrow and hardening arteries
(4) narrowing arteries and hard arteries
(5) narrowing, hard arteries

① ② ③ ④ ⑤

12. Sentence 4: **This condition does not allowing the heart to receive the blood it needs for healthy functioning.**

Which correction should be made to sentence 4?

(1) change does to doesn't
(2) change allowing to allow
(3) change receive to receiving
(4) change functioning to function
(5) no correction is necessary

① ② ③ ④ ⑤

13. Sentence 6: **Avoiding the complications that come with heart disease such as chest pain, stroke, or heart attack, a healthy heart is possible through diet.**

Which is the best way to write the underlined portion of sentence 6? If the original is the best way, choose option (1).

(1) a healthy heart is possible through diet
(2) heart health is dependent on diet
(3) is possible if you keep your heart healthy through diet
(4) diet is connected to heart health
(5) a healthy diet yields a healthy heart

① ② ③ ④ ⑤

14. Sentence 9: **You should only eat the so-called "good" fats polyunsaturated and monounsaturated.**

Where should the modifier *only* be placed in sentence 9?

(1) after fats
(2) before polyunsaturated
(3) after monounsaturated
(4) after eat
(5) no correction is necessary

① ② ③ ④ ⑤

15. Sentence 11: **There are several foods that you should limit or avoid to keep your heart healthy.**

Which correction should be made to sentence 11?

(1) move heart to follow healthy
(2) move several to follow foods
(3) replace or with and
(4) remove that you
(5) no correction is necessary

① ② ③ ④ ⑤

UNIT 3

LL COOL J

By achieving his GED, LL Cool J has made some of his dreams a reality.

L Cool J is a man of many talents. Whether as a recording artist, actor, writer, clothing designer, or fitness expert, the man formerly known as James Todd Smith has made his mark on society. Born on Long Island, New York, LL Cool J (*Ladies Love Cool James*) spent much of his youth participating in the Boy Scouts and singing in the church choir. At age 16, he began to record and send songs to various record companies.

One of those companies, Def Jam Records, released his first album in 1984, around the time that hip-hop and rap music were beginning to grow popular. LL Cool J left high school to record the album, which sold more than 100,000 copies and helped establish him as a rising talent in the music industry. He later earned his GED certificate, the importance of which he references in his song *Say What*.

Over the course of his lengthy career, LL Cool J became the first rap artist to have 10 straight platinum-selling albums. His musical fame provided him with the opportunity to explore other ventures, such as acting and writing. LL Cool J once said,

> **❝ I think when you move past your fear and you go after your dreams wholeheartedly, you become free. ❞**

LL Cool J helped launch two clothing lines, FUBU and Todd Smith. He also created an online social networking community for aspiring artists.

BIO BLAST: LL Cool J

- Born James Todd Smith on January 14, 1968, on Long Island, New York
- Won two Grammy Awards for his music
- Wrote *LL Cool J's Platinum Workout*, a *New York Times* best-seller
- Starred on various television shows and appeared in more than 30 films
- Wrote the children's book *And the Winner Is*, about a young basketball player learning sportsmanship

Unit 4: Usage

In the same way that a chef uses specific ingredients when cooking, you use specific types of words when writing. Think of nouns, verbs, and subjects as the ingredients you need to form a sentence. In Unit 4, you will learn how to use different types of words, and modify them to show the time in which actions or conditions occur. Take a moment to familiarize yourself with the following glossary of terms, noting the examples provided. These terms will appear throughout the book.

GLOSSARY OF TERMS

Object: Someone or something that receives or completes the subject's action: *Mary jumps rope*.

Possessive: A word or form of a word that indicates ownership: *Mary's jump rope*.

Singular: A word or form of a word indicating one person or thing: *one car; a book*.

Plural: A word or form of a word indicating more than one person or thing: *two cars; four books*.

First-person narrative: Text that is written from the *I* point of view: *I borrowed his car*.

Second-person narrative: Text that is written from the *you* point of view: *You borrowed his car*.

Third-person narrative: Text that is written from the *he/she/it* point of view: *She borrowed his car*.

Antecedent: A subject that is replaced by a pronoun: *When Mary thought of George, she called him* (*Mary* and *George* are replaced by *she* and *him*).

Participles: A modification of verbs that indicates tense: *given; written; brought; taken*.

Suffix: An ending that is added to a word to change its tense or function. For example, *–ed* and *–ing*.

Prefix: A small unit of letters added to the beginning of a word to change its meaning. For example, *un-*, *pre-*, and *dis-*: <u>un</u>happy, <u>pre</u>existing, <u>dis</u>satisfied.

Syllable: A unit of measure in spoken language: *syl*la*ble* has three syllables.

Compound subjects: When two or more subjects are joined by *and* or *or*: *Uncle Joe and Aunt Mary; the boy or girl*.

Table of Contents

Nouns

usage
he
she it
were
is

① Learn the Skill

Nouns are parts of speech that represent people, places, or things and are often the subject of sentences (*mom*; *Ohio*; *map*). Understanding how to correctly use and identify nouns will make your writing stronger and help you answer questions on the editing portion of the GED Language Arts/Writing Test.

② Practice the Skill

By mastering the skill of identifying nouns, you will improve your writing and test-taking skills, especially as they relate to the GED Language Arts/Writing Test. Read the paragraph and strategies below. Then answer the question that follows.

A A noun that represents the name of a person, a title, or a specific place is a proper noun: *Mrs. Morgan*. Proper nouns are always capitalized. You will learn more about capitalization in Unit 5. Like other nouns, proper nouns can be made up of more than one word.

B Nouns can appear in different places within sentences. The words *obligations* and *kids* are nouns that appear at the end of sentences 3 and 4. *Message* is a noun that appears in the middle of sentence 5.

(A)

A (1) "When you say no, mean it," mrs. morgan, my former u.s. history teacher, laughed as she brushed a strand of reddish-blond hair from her eyes. (2) We were standing together in the hallway outside one wing of my old school. (3) The warm afternoon sun kept us from other **B** obligations. (4) "That's one thing I always tried to do with my **B** kids. (5) I didn't want to send the **B** message that I didn't mean what I said. (6) If people think you don't mean what you say, they will take advantage of you," she finished, giving me a motherly look. (7) Although I didn't know it at the time, this piece of advice would change my life in a positive way.

TEST-TAKING TIPS

Identify nouns by first looking for people, places, or things in sentences. Things can also be ideas or concepts in addition to physical things. Subjects of sentences that come before verbs are likely nouns. Identify proper nouns by looking for names of people, places, or titles.

1. Sentence 1: **"When you say no, mean it,"** <u>mrs. morgan, my former u.s. history teacher,</u> **laughed as she brushed a strand of reddish-blond hair from her eyes.**

   Which is the best way to write the underlined portion of sentence 1? If the original is the best way, choose option (1).

   (1) mrs. morgan, my former u.s. history teacher
   (2) Mrs. morgan, my former u.s. history teacher
   (3) Mrs. Morgan, my former u.s. history teacher
   (4) Mrs. Morgan, my former U.S. history teacher
   (5) Mrs. Morgan, my former U.S. History teacher

Directions: Choose the one best answer to each question.

Questions 2 and 3 refer to the following paragraph.

(1) After I learned about my grandmother's childhood adventures in Europe, I admired her more than ever. (2) We looked through her photo albums together, and she showed me pictures from when she was young. (3) We laughed as she told me stories about her journeys all over italy, spain, and france. (4) She visited the Eiffel Tower when she was only 5 years old. (6) I couldn't believe how young she looked, and that the people standing beside her were her parents. (7) Grandmother's parents looked so strong and dignified.

2. Sentence 3: **We laughed as she told me stories about her journeys all over italy, spain, and france.**

   Which is the best way to write the underlined portion of sentence 3? If the original is the best way, choose option (1).

   (1) stories about her journeys all over italy, spain, and france
   (2) stories about her journeys all over Italy, Spain, and France
   (3) stories about her Journeys all over Italy, Spain, and france
   (4) stories about her Journeys all over Italy, Spain, and France
   (5) Stories about Her Journeys all over Italy, Spain, and France

3. Sentence 4: **She visited the Eiffel Tower when she was only 5 years old.**

   Which of the following words from sentence 4 is a noun?

   (1) only
   (2) visited
   (3) Eiffel Tower
   (4) when
   (5) old

Questions 4 and 5 refer to the following paragraph.

(1) There are several different ways to find information in a public library. (2) A library's catalog lists Books and other materials that the library owns. (3) Many library catalogs are now available on the Internet. (4) Whatever kind of catalog system your library has, it will provide the information you need to identify the book you want and find it on the shelf.

4. Sentence 2: **A library's catalog lists Books and other materials that the library owns.**

   Which correction should be made to sentence 2?

   (1) change Books to books
   (2) change library to Library
   (3) change catalogs to Catalogs
   (4) change materials to Materials
   (5) no correction is necessary

5. Sentence 4: **Whatever kind of catalog system your library has, it will provide the information you need to identify the book you want and find it on the shelf.**

   Which is the best way to write the underlined portion of sentence 4? If the original is the best way, choose option (1).

   (1) identify the book you want and find it on the shelf
   (2) identify the what you want and find it on the shelf
   (3) identify the Book you want and find it on the shelf
   (4) identify the Book you want and find It on the Shelf
   (5) identify the book and find it On the Shelf

Pronouns

usage
he
she   it
were
is

① Learn the Skill

Pronouns are words that take the place of other nouns in sentences. Pronouns take different forms depending on how they are used. The different forms of pronouns are subject, object, and possessive. Subject pronouns—such as *I*, *she*, and *he*—are used as subjects in sentences. Object pronouns—such as *me*, *you*, and *him*—often follow verbs. Possessive pronouns—such as *his*, *hers*, *ours*, and *theirs*—are used to show possession.

② Practice the Skill

By mastering the skill of using pronouns, you will improve your writing and test-taking skills, especially as they relate to the GED Language Arts/Writing Test. Read the paragraphs and strategies below. Then answer the question that follows.

A In sentence 1, *him* is an object pronoun because it follows the verb *told* and has taken the place of *Uncle Joe* (the object of the verb).

B In sentence 2, *he* is a subject pronoun because it has taken the place of the subject of the sentence: *Uncle Joe.* Other subject pronouns include *I, she, you,* and *it.*

(C)

A (1) I'm sure that <u>Uncle Joe</u> remembered the time that I <u>told him</u> I didn't want to spend three weeks with Uncle Joe and Aunt Mary during my vacation. (2) However, <u>he</u> **B** talked me into making the visit, and I ended up having a great time. (3) I'd said "No" and then changed my mind a dozen times in response to Uncle Joe's requests. (4) Uncle Joe had no reason to think that this time would be any different.

(D)

(5) It was time to put my thoughts into action. (6) At the end of the day, I dialed Uncle Joe's telephone number. (7) I told Uncle Joe that I appreciated the offer of work, but I had other plans. (8) I said that I knew Uncle Joe was probably disappointed, but I would not change my mind.

✔ TEST-TAKING TIPS

The following chart lists subject and object pronouns and the possessive forms of each. These can be singular or plural as well.

Pronoun Form		Subject	Object	Possessive
Singular		I, you, she, he, it	me, you, her, him, it	my, mine, yours, hers, his, its, ours, theirs
Plural		we, you, they	us, you, them	our, ours, your, yours, their, theirs

1. Sentence 7: **I told Uncle Joe that I appreciated the offer of work, but I had other plans.**

   Which correction should be made to sentence 7?

   (1) replace <u>Uncle Joe</u> with <u>his</u>
   (2) change <u>Uncle Joe</u> to <u>uncle joe</u>
   (3) replace <u>Uncle Joe</u> with <u>I</u>
   (4) replace <u>Uncle Joe</u> with <u>him</u>
   (5) change <u>Uncle Joe</u> to <u>Joe</u>

<u>Directions</u>: Choose the <u>one best answer</u> to each question.

<u>Questions 2 and 3</u> refer to the following paragraph.

(1) After I learned about my grandmother's childhood adventures, I admired grandmother more than ever. (2) Grandmother and I looked through grandmother's photo albums together and grandmother showed me pictures from when she was young. (3) I couldn't believe how young grandmother looked, and that the people standing beside grandmother were grandmother's parents. (4) Grandmother's parents looked so strong and dignified.

2. Sentence 2: **Grandmother and I looked through <u>grandmother's photo albums together and grandmother showed me pictures</u> from when she was young.**

    Which is the best way to write the underlined portion of sentence 2? If the original is the best way, choose option (1).

    (1) grandmother's photo albums together and grandmother showed me pictures
    (2) her photo albums together and she showed me pictures
    (3) her photo albums together and it showed me pictures
    (4) she photo albums together and her showed me pictures
    (5) their photo albums together and she showed me pictures

3. Sentence 4: **Grandmother's parents looked so strong and dignified.**

    Which correction should be made to sentence 4?

    (1) change <u>parents</u> to <u>Parents</u>
    (2) change <u>Grandmother's parents</u> to <u>They</u>
    (3) change <u>Grandmother's</u> to <u>She</u>
    (4) change <u>parents</u> to <u>mom and dad</u>
    (5) change <u>Grandmother's</u> to <u>My</u>

<u>Questions 4 and 5</u> refer to the following paragraphs.

(A)
(1) My friends and I all enjoy a good baseball or basketball game, but in my opinion, professional sports today are too violent. (2) If you don't believe it, look at the way hockey players behave. (3) Hockey players often stop skating to fight with the other team!

(B)
(4) I think the use of violence for entertainment is dangerous to our society. (5) Not only are the players violent, but fans can become violent, too. (6) I watch fans get worked up after a referee misses a call or the fans' team loses. (7) The fans become dangerous mobs looking for trouble after the game ends, or even while it is still being played.

4. Sentence 2: **<u>If you don't believe it</u>, look at the way hockey players behave.**

    Which is the best way to write the underlined portion of sentence 2? If the original is the best way, choose option (1).

    (1) If you don't believe it
    (2) If they don't believe it
    (3) If I don't believe you
    (4) If you don't believe him
    (5) If we don't believe them

5. Sentence 6: **I watch fans get worked up after a referee misses a call or the fans' team loses.**

    Which correction should be made to sentence 6?

    (1) replace <u>fans</u> with <u>referees</u>
    (2) change <u>a referee</u> to <u>he</u>
    (3) change <u>fans</u> to <u>they</u>
    (4) change <u>fans</u> to <u>them</u>
    (5) no correction is necessary

Pronoun Agreement

1 Learn the Skill

Pronoun agreement helps you properly use pronouns. Pronouns must agree in number, gender, and point-of-view with the nouns that come before them. The word or words for which a pronoun stands is called the **antecedent**. Antecedents usually appear in the same sentence before a pronoun, but sometimes they can appear in a previous sentence.

2 Practice the Skill

By mastering the skill of using proper pronoun agreement, you will improve your writing and test-taking skills, especially as they relate to the GED Language Arts/Writing Test. Read the paragraphs and strategies below. Then answer the question that follows.

A In sentence 2, *Uncle Joe* and *Aunt Mary* function as antecedents for the pronoun *them* in sentence 3.

B The plural pronoun *they* in sentence 7 agrees with the plural antecedent *words* that appears earlier in the sentence. A singular pronoun needs to have a singular antecedent, and a plural pronoun needs to have a plural antecedent.

(D)
(1) It was time to put my thoughts into action. (2) At the end of the day, I called Uncle Joe and Aunt Mary. (3) I told them that I appreciated the offer of work, but I had other plans. (4) I said that I knew they were probably disappointed, but I would not change my mind. (5) Surprisingly, Uncle Joe and Aunt Mary said they understood. (6) Then she told me that they supported my decision.

(E)
(7) Although Mrs. Morgan's words were simple, they were valuable. (8) She taught me the importance of matching my words with my thoughts. (9) By following this advice, I gained self-confidence. (10) Now, I control my own future by choosing my words carefully. (11) I say what I mean, and I get what I want.

✓ TEST-TAKING TIPS

It's easy to misuse the pronoun *they* in order to avoid mentioning a particular gender: *A person must do whatever they feel is right* should be *A person must do whatever he or she feels is right*. Pronouns must agree in terms of gender. If you are referring to a female, you should use the female pronoun *she*. If you are referring to a male, you should use the male pronoun *he*. If you are referring to an object with a neutral gender, you should use the pronoun *it*.

1. Sentence 6: **Then <u>she told me</u> that they supported my decision.**

   Which is the best way to write the underlined portion of sentence 6? If the original is the best way, choose option (1).

   (1) she told me
   (2) he told me
   (3) they told me
   (4) it told me
   (5) you told me

③ Apply the Skill

Directions: Choose the <u>one best answer</u> to each question.

<u>Questions 2 and 3</u> refer to the following letter.

> To Whom It May Concern,
>
>   (1) I am writing to oppose the school dress code that the school board has recently proposed. (2) A dress code not only tells kids what to wear to school, they limit their ability to tell other people about their interests, opinions, and ideas. (3) A dress code is an easy way for school officials to get rid of ideas we don't like.

2. Sentence 2: **A dress code not only tells kids what to wear to school, they limit their ability to tell other people about their interests, opinions, and ideas.**

    Which correction should be made to sentence 2?

    (1) replace <u>limit</u> with <u>restrict</u>
    (2) change the first <u>their</u> to <u>your</u>
    (3) remove the comma after <u>school</u>
    (4) change <u>they limit</u> to <u>it limits</u>
    (5) replace <u>other people</u> with <u>them</u>

3. Sentence 3: **A dress code is an easy way for school officials to get rid of ideas <u>we don't like.</u>**

    Which is the best way to write the underlined portion of sentence 3? If the original is the best way, choose option (1).

    (1) we don't like
    (2) they don't like
    (3) it doesn't like
    (4) I don't like
    (5) she doesn't like

<u>Questions 4 and 5</u> refer to the following paragraph.

>   (1) Some modern composers write classical music. (2) Other composers write popular music. (3) Most composers, however, use a system called musical notation to write our melodies and harmonies. (4) Special papers are used with sets of lines running across the page. (5) Composers place symbols on the paper called notes. (6) The notes show at what pitches the music should be played.

4. Sentence 3: **Most composers, however, use a system called musical notation to write our melodies and harmonies.**

    Which correction should be made to sentence 3?

    (1) remove the <u>comma</u> after <u>however</u>
    (2) change <u>musical notation</u> to <u>Musical Notation</u>
    (3) change <u>our</u> to <u>their</u>
    (4) change <u>our</u> to <u>them</u>
    (5) no correction is necessary

5. Sentence 4: **<u>Special papers are used with sets of lines</u> running across the page.**

    Which is the best way to write the underlined portion of sentence 4? If the original is the best way, choose option (1).

    (1) Special papers are used with sets of lines
    (2) Composers are used to special papers with sets of lines
    (3) Special papers with sets of lines are used
    (4) They use special papers with sets of lines
    (5) Composers use a special paper with a line

UNIT 4

Collective Nouns

① **Learn the Skill**

Collective nouns refer to a group of people, animals, or things. Some collective nouns take singular verbs, while other collective nouns take plural verbs. For example, if a collective noun is considered a single unit that acts as a whole, such as a *company of soldiers*, it takes a singular verb. If a collective noun has parts that can act differently, such as *members*, it takes a plural verb: *The group members gather for the meeting.*

② **Practice the Skill**

By mastering the skill of using collective nouns, you will improve your writing and test-taking skills, especially as they relate to the GED Language Arts/Writing Test. Read the paragraph and strategies below. Then answer the question that follows.

Ⓐ The words *company* and *family* in sentence 3 are collective nouns because each refers to a singular group of people. All of Uncle Joe's family lives in Little Rock, and the company as a whole is offering a job to the writer.

Ⓑ The collective noun *family* in sentence 8 takes a plural verb because it is broken up into parts, or *members*. The *family members* might have different expectations about the writer's potential visit and therefore might respond differently.

(C)

(1) Mrs. Morgan is right, I need to say no and mean it. (2) Uncle Joe wants me to move to Little Rock. (3) Little Rock is where his **Ⓐ**family lives, and he says his plumbing **Ⓐ**company has work for me. (4) I've said "No" to his previous requests, but he keeps pushing the issue. (5) I'm sure that he remembers the time I didn't want to spend three weeks with his family during my vacation. (6) However, he talked me into making the visit, and the group always have a great time. (7) I've said "No" and then changed my mind a dozen times in response to his family's requests. (8) The **Ⓑ**members of his **Ⓑ**family have no reason to think that this time will be any different.

☑ TEST-TAKING TIPS

Use collective nouns when writing about groups made up of more than one person or thing. Sometimes a verb that follows a collective noun may sound wrong, such as *the herd of buffalo has moved on*, even though it's grammatically correct.

1. Sentence 6: **However, he talked me into making the visit, and the group always have a great time.**

   Which correction should be made to sentence 6?

   (1) change <u>group</u> to <u>group's</u>
   (2) change <u>have</u> to <u>has</u>
   (3) change <u>me</u> to <u>my</u>
   (4) change <u>time</u> to <u>times</u>
   (5) no correction is necessary

Directions: Choose the <u>one best answer</u> to each question.

<u>Questions 2 and 3</u> refer to the following paragraphs.

(A)

(1) My friends and I enjoy a good baseball or basketball game, but in my opinion professional sports today are too violent. (2) If you don't believe it, look at the way hockey teams behave. (3) The team often stop skating to fight with the other team!

(B)

(4) I think that the use of violence for entertainment is dangerous to our society. (5) Not only are the players violent, but fans can become violent, too. (6) I watch fans get worked up after the referees miss a call or their team lose. (7) They become dangerous mobs looking for trouble after the game ends, or even while it is still being played.

---

2. Sentence 3: **<u>The team often stop skating</u> to fight with the other team!**

    Which is the best way to write the underlined portion of sentence 3? If the original is the best way, choose option (1).

    (1) The team often stop skating
    (2) The teams often stops skating
    (3) The team's often stop skating
    (4) The team often stopped skating
    (5) The team often stops skating

3. Sentence 6: **I watch fans get worked up after the referees miss a call or their team lose.**

    Which correction should be made to sentence 6?

    (1) change <u>miss</u> to <u>misses</u>
    (2) change <u>get</u> to <u>gets</u>
    (3) change <u>call</u> to <u>calls</u>
    (4) change <u>lose</u> to <u>loses</u>
    (5) no correction is necessary

<u>Questions 4 and 5</u> refer to the following paragraphs.

(A)

(1) Have you ever watched a group of cats play outside? (2) Typically, the cats play by themselves. (3) One will chase a butterfly, while another uses a wooden fence as a balance beam. (4) After an hour or so of running around, the group come inside. (5) Some of the group heads for their food bowls, while some of the group meow for attention.

(B)

(6) It's often hard to know what a group of cats wants. (7) Some of the group might perch on windowsills in the living room to watch for birds outside. (8) Some of the group might settle down for an afternoon nap. (9) It's clear that even in a group, cats like to do their own thing.

---

4. Sentence 4: **After an hour or so of running around, the group come inside.**

    Which correction should be made to sentence 4?

    (1) change <u>running</u> to <u>runs</u>
    (2) change <u>hour</u> to <u>Hour</u>
    (3) change <u>come</u> to <u>comes</u>
    (4) change <u>group</u> to <u>groups</u>
    (5) no correction is necessary

5. Sentence 6: **It's often hard to know what a group of cats wants.**

    Which correction should be made to sentence 6?

    (1) insert a comma after <u>know</u>
    (2) change <u>cats</u> to <u>cat</u>
    (3) change <u>know</u> to <u>knows</u>
    (4) change <u>wants</u> to <u>want</u>
    (5) no correction is necessary

UNIT 4

Simple Verb Tense

usage
he
she it
were
is

① Learn the Skill

Verbs have different forms called tenses. **Simple verb tense** shows whether an action takes place or a condition exists in the past, present, or future. As a writer, the tenses of the verbs you use clearly demonstrate when something happened or when a condition existed: *We made a snowman* (action); *It snowed yesterday* (condition). It's important to use consistent verb tenses in order to eliminate confusion about the time or order in which events happen.

② Practice the Skill

By mastering the skill of using simple verb tenses, you will improve your writing and test-taking skills, especially as they relate to the GED Language Arts/Writing Test. Read the paragraphs and strategies below. Then answer the question that follows.

A Past tense verbs such as *told* and *had* in sentence 3 indicate that the conversation with Uncle Joe has already taken place. The past tense is shown by changing the spelling of the verb *tell* to *told* and the verb *have* to *had*. Future tense is indicated by placing a helping verb, such as *will*, in front of the regular verb: *will tell*.

B The past tense verb *taught* in sentence 7 indicates that paragraph E is written in past tense. However, the use of the verbs *control* in sentence 9 and *say* in sentence 10 indicate present tense. The writer has changed tenses in the paragraph, switching from past tense to present tense in order to make his or her point.

(D)

(1) It was time to put my thoughts into action. (2) At the end of the day, I dialed Uncle Joe's telephone number. (3) I <u>told</u> him that I appreciated the offer of work, but I had other plans. (4) I said that I know he was probably disappointed, but I would not change my mind.
(5) Surprisingly, Uncle Joe said that he understood and that he supported my decision.

(E)

(6) Although Mrs. Morgan's advice was simple, it was valuable. (7) She <u>taught</u> me the importance of matching my words with my thoughts. (8) By following this advice, I gained self-confidence. (9) Now, I <u>control</u> my own future by choosing my words carefully. (10) I <u>say</u> what I mean, and I get what I want.

☑ TEST-TAKING TIPS

When you write, try not to switch tenses within the same sentence. You can switch to another tense in the next sentence or the next paragraph if you choose.

1. Sentence 4: **I said that I know he was probably disappointed, but I would not change my mind.**

   Which correction should be made to sentence 4?

   (1) change <u>said</u> to <u>say</u>
   (2) change <u>know</u> to <u>knew</u>
   (3) replace <u>was</u> with <u>is</u>
   (4) change <u>disappointed</u> to <u>will disappoint</u>
   (5) no correction is necessary

UNIT 4

Directions: Choose the <u>one best answer</u> to each question.

<u>Questions 2 and 3</u> refer to the following paragraph.

> (1) There were several different ways to find information in a public library. (2) A library's catalog lists books and other materials that the library owns. (3) Many library catalogs are now available on the Internet. (4) Whatever kind of catalog system your library has, it provide you with the information you need to identify the books you want and to find them on the shelves.

2. Sentence 1: **There were several different ways to find information in a public library.**

   Which correction should be made to sentence 1?

   (1) change <u>were</u> to <u>are</u>
   (●) replace <u>find</u> with <u>found</u>
   (3) change <u>were</u> to <u>is</u>
   (4) replace <u>find</u> with <u>will find</u>
   (5) no correction is necessary

3. Sentence 4: **Whatever kind of catalog system your library has, <u>it provide you with the information you need</u> to identify the books you want and to find them on the shelves.**

   Which is the best way to write the underlined portion of sentence 4? If the original is the best way, choose option (1).

   (1) it provide you with the information you need
   (2) they provide you with the information you need
   (③) it will provide you with the information you need
   (4) it provides us with the information you need
   (5) it provide you with the information you will need

<u>Questions 4 and 5</u> refer to the following paragraph.

> (1) Do you like action movies? (2) Well, get ready, because the biggest action movie of all time will be opening in theaters on May 20th! (3) If you like explosions, car chases, and hair-raising escapes, this was the movie for you! (4) We've spent millions of dollars making this movie, and we promise that it will not disappoint you! (5) It includes some of the biggest stars in Hollywood, and some of the best special effects you see! (6) So mark your calendars. (7) May 20th will be the first day to see the greatest action movie ever made.

4. Sentence 3: **If you like explosions, car chases, and hair-raising escapes, this was the movie for you!**

   Which correction should be made to sentence 3?

   (1) change <u>was</u> to <u>is</u>
   (2) change <u>was</u> to <u>are</u>
   (3) replace <u>like</u> to <u>will like</u>
   (4) change <u>was</u> to <u>will be</u>
   (5) no correction is necessary

5. Sentence 5: **It includes some of the biggest stars in Hollywood, and <u>some of the best special effects you see</u>!**

   Which is the best way to write the underlined portion of sentence 5? If the original is the best way, choose option (1).

   (1) some of the best special effects you see
   (2) some of the best special effects you seen
   (3) some of the best special effects I will see
   (④) some of the best special effects you will see
   (5) some of the best special effects you saw

Regular Verb Tense

Usage
he
she it
were
is

① Learn the Skill

Regular verb tenses show an action that is taking place or a condition that exists in the past or present. They are made by changing the endings of regular verbs. A **suffix**, such as *-ed*, *-s*, and *-ing*, must be added (*practiced*; *practices*; *practicing*) to form past (*-ed*) and present (*-s* and *-ing*) tenses, or participles. In some cases, a letter at the end of a regular verb must be changed, dropped, or doubled to create the new verb tense. For example, to change a verb that ends with *y* to past or present tense, you must follow this rule: if the letter before the *y* is a consonant, change the *y* to an *i*: *copy* = *cop<u>ied</u>* and *cop<u>ies</u>*. If the letter before the *y* is a vowel, keep the *y*: *play* = *pla<u>yed</u>* and *pla<u>ys</u>*.

② Practice the Skill

By mastering the skill of using regular verb tenses, you will improve your writing and test-taking skills, especially as they relate to the GED Language Arts/Writing Test. Read the paragraphs and strategies below. Then answer the question that follows.

A Notice *to do* and *to send* in sentences 4 and 5. When *to* precedes a verb, the verb is in its original state (base form). The *to+verb* combination does not carry a tense and therefore should never have a suffix: *to ~~running~~; to ~~played~~; to ~~sings~~*. The verb or verb phrase that precedes *to+verb* carries the tense in the sentence.

B In sentence 8 *nod = nodded* and *grab = grabbing*. The last letters of these words are doubled because, in English, the rule is that if the word is one syllable, you double the last letter before adding a suffix that begins with a vowel. If a word has more than one syllable, sound out the word and, if the emphasis is on the end of the word, double the last letter: *control = controlled* and *controlling*.

✓ TEST-TAKING TIPS

A good rule to remember is: remove the *e* at the end of a word when adding a suffix that begins in a vowel: *hope = hop<u>ed</u>* and *hop<u>ing</u>*.

(A)

(1) "When you say no, mean it," Mrs. Morgan, my former U.S. History teacher, laughed as she brushed a strand of reddish-blond hair from her eyes. (2) We were standing together in the hallway outside one wing of my old school. (3) The warm afternoon sun kept us from other obligations. (4) "That's one thing I always tried <u>to do</u> with my kids. (5) I didn't want <u>to send</u> the message that I didn't mean what I said. (6) If people think you don't mean what you say, they will take advantage of you," she finished, giving me a motherly look. (7) Although I didn't know it at the time, this piece of advice would change my life in a positive way.

(B)

(8) "You're right," I <u>nodded</u>, <u>grabbing</u> my gym bag and heading toward the open door of the gymnasium. (9) I sat on the bleacher beside my best friend Kayla. (10) When I retrieve my clothes out of my bag, I saw the crinkled letter from my uncle.

1. Sentence 10: **When I retrieve my homework out of my backpack, I saw the crinkled letter from my uncle.**

   Which correction should be made to sentence 10?

   (1) change <u>retrieve</u> to <u>retrieved</u>
   (2) change <u>letter</u> to <u>Letter</u>
   (3) replace <u>retrieve</u> with <u>retrieving</u>
   (4) change <u>crinkled</u> to <u>crinkle</u>
   (5) no correction is necessary

Directions: Choose the one best answer to each question.

Questions 2 and 3 refer to the following paragraph.

(1) After I learned about my grandmother's childhood adventures, I admired her more than ever. (2) We looked through grandmother's photo albums together and she is showing me pictures from when she was young. (3) I couldn't believe how young grandmother looked, and that the people stand beside her were her parents. (4) They looked so strong and dignified.

2. Sentence 2: **We looked through grandmother's photo albums together and she is showing me pictures from when she was young.**

   Which is the best way to write the underlined portion of sentence 2? If the original is the best way, choose option (1).

   (1) she is showing me pictures
   (2) she shows me pictures
   (3) she was showing me the picture
   (4) she wanted to show me pictures
   (5) she showed me pictures

3. Sentence 3: **I couldn't believe how young grandmother looked, and that the people stand beside her were her parents.**

   Which correction should be made to sentence 3?

   (1) change looked to look
   (2) replace believe with believed
   (3) change stand to standing
   (4) change were to was
   (5) no correction is necessary

Questions 4 and 5 refer to the following paragraph.

(1) Thank you for purchasing your new cell phone. (2) Your new phone is also a radio transmitter and receiver. (3) It was designed and manufactured not to exceed certain limits set by the U.S. Government. (4) The guidelines were base on standards that were developed by scientists. (5) The scientists tested the phones to make sure they are safe for everyone who is using them. (6) You will receive more information about your new phone's safeguards in the mail within a few weeks.

4. Sentence 4: **The guidelines were base on standards that were developed by scientists.**

   Which correction should be made to sentence 4?

   (1) change guidelines to Guidelines
   (2) replace base with bassed
   (3) change were developed to are developed
   (4) change base to based
   (5) no correction is necessary

5. Sentence 6: **You will receive more information about your new phone's safeguards in the mail within a few weeks.**

   Which is the best way to write the underlined portion of sentence 6? If the original is the best way, choose option (1).

   (1) You will receive more information
   (2) You received more information
   (3) You are to receive more information
   (4) You receive more information
   (5) You are receiving more information

Perfect Verb Tense

usage
he
she *it*
were
is

① Learn the Skill

Perfect verb tense describes actions at many different points in time. **Past perfect tense** describes an action that took place before another action. It is formed by using *had* in front of the main verb: *They had gone swimming.* **Present perfect tense** describes an event that began in the past and continues in the present. It is formed by using *has, have,* or *have been* in front of the main verb: *They have been swimming for hours.* **Future perfect tense** describes an event that will happen in the future. It is formed by placing *will have* or *will have been* in front of a verb ending in *–ing*: *By dinner they will have been swimming all day.*

② Practice the Skill

By mastering the skill of using perfect verb tense, you will improve your writing and test-taking skills, especially as they relate to the GED Language Arts/Writing Test. Read the paragraph and strategies below. Then answer the question that follows.

A *Uncle Joe has been wanting* in sentence 2 is an example of present perfect tense because Joe's been wanting the writer to move to Little Rock *for a long time,* not just in the present moment.

B *I had said no* in sentence 3 is an example of past perfect tense because the writer said no to Uncle Joe every time he asked the writer to move.

(C)
(1) Mrs. Morgan was right, I needed to say no and mean it. (2) **A** <u>Uncle Joe has been wanting</u> me to move to Little Rock to work for him in his plumbing shop **A** <u>for a long time</u>. (3) **B** <u>I had said no</u> to his previous requests, but he kept pushing the issue. (4) I'm sure that he remembered the time that I told him that I didn't want to spend three weeks with him and Aunt Mary during my vacation. (5) However, I will have been letting my uncle talk me into making the visit, and I ended up having a great time. (6) I'd said no and then changed my mind a dozen times in response to Uncle Joe's requests. (7) He had no reason to think that this time would be any different.

✓ TEST-TAKING TIPS

Carefully read each sentence and be sure to identify the intended tenses. Look for key words, such as *had, have,* and *will,* and verb endings, such as *–ing* and *–ed.*

1. Sentence 5: **However, I will have been letting my uncle talk me into making the visit, and I ended up having a great time.**

Which is the best way to write the underlined portion of sentence 5? If the original is the best way, choose option (1).

(1) However, I will have been letting my uncle
(2) However, I had let my uncle
(3) However, I have let my uncle
(4) However, I will have let my uncle
(5) However, I letting my uncle

UNIT 4

Questions 4 and 5 refer to the following paragraph.

Directions: Choose the one best answer to each question.

Questions 2 and 3 refer to the following paragraph.

(1) Have you ever watched a group of cats play outside? (2) After they had run around for an hour or so, the group comes inside. (3) Some of the group head for their food bowls, while some of the group meow for attention. (4) It's often hard to predict what a group of cats will do. (5) Before dinner, you might find that some of the group had perched on windowsills in the living room all afternoon to watch for birds. (6) Others in the group napping for hours. (7) It's clear that even in a group, cats like to do their own thing.

(1) There's a simple way to get the best price on a new car. (2) If you follow this simple, 3-step system, you can save thousands of dollars on your next car. (3) Step 1 is to find out what the dealer have paid for the car. (4) Step 2 is to ask whether the dealer has received a hidden rebate for the car. (5) By the end of last year, dealers has receive all kinds of rebates from car makers. (6) They will try to keep these rebates hidden from you during the deal! (7) Step 3 is to ask the dealer what his employees pay for a car. (8) Once you know these things, you can bargain with any dealer.

2. Sentence 2: **After they had run around for an hour or so, the group comes inside.**

    Which correction should be made to sentence 2?

    (1) insert a comma after around
    (2) replace had with have
    (3) replace comes with come
    (4) replace had with will
    (5) no correction is necessary

3. Sentence 6: **Others in the group napping for hours.**

    Which correction should be made to sentence 6?

    (1) insert had after group
    (2) change napping to had napped
    (3) insert will have been after group
    (4) change hours to Hours
    (5) no correction is necessary

4. Sentence 3: **Step 1 is to find out what the dealer have paid for the car.**

    Which is the best way to write the underlined portion of sentence 3? If the original is the best way, choose option (1).

    (1) what the dealer have paid for the car
    (2) what the dealer pay for the car
    (3) what the dealer had paid for the car
    (4) what the dealer will have paid for the car
    (5) what the dealer will be paying for the car

5. Sentence 5: **By the end of last year, dealers has receive all kinds of rebates from car makers.**

    Which is the best way to write the underlined portion of sentence 5? If the original is the best way, choose option (1).

    (1) dealers has receive
    (2) dealers have received
    (3) dealers had receiving
    (4) dealers will have been receiving
    (5) dealers had received

Irregular Verbs

Usage
he
she it
were
is

① Learn the Skill

Irregular verbs do not always follow verb tense rules. In a few cases, the past tense and past participle forms of an irregular verb are spelled the same, such as *brought* and *said*. However, in most cases they are spelled differently. The best way to learn irregular verb forms is to memorize them.

② Practice the Skill

By mastering the skill of using irregular verbs, you will improve your writing and test-taking skills, especially as they relate to the GED Language Arts/Writing Test. Read the paragraphs and strategies below. Then answer the question that follows.

Ⓐ In sentence 1, the irregular verb *chose* is the past tense form of the verb *choose*. In sentence 8, the irregular verb *took* is the past tense form of the verb *take*.

Ⓑ In sentence 7, *taught* is both the past tense form and the past participle form of the verb *teach*. In sentence 10, *given* is both the past tense form and the past participle form of the verb *give*. The use of *have been* before *given* is a clue that is it a past participle.

(D)

(1) I **Ⓐ** <u>chose</u> to put my thoughts into action. (2) At the end of the day, I dialed Uncle Joe's telephone number. (3) I told him I appreciated the offer of work, but I had other plans. (4) I said that I knew he was probably disappointed, but I would not change my mind. (5) Surprisingly, Uncle Joe say that he understood and that he supported my decision.

(E)

(6) Although Mrs. Morgan's advice was simple, it was valuable. (7) She **Ⓑ** <u>taught</u> me the importance of matching my words with my thoughts. (8) I **Ⓐ** <u>took</u> this advice and I gained self-confidence. (9) Now, I control my own future by choosing my words carefully. (10) I say what I mean, and I **Ⓑ** <u>have been given</u> what I want.

☑ TEST-TAKING TIPS

The following chart lists some common irregular verbs. Remember, the past participle form is always used with a helping verb such as *has*, *had*, or *have*.

Irregular Verb	Past Tense	Past Participle
begin	began	have begun
do	did	have done
give	gave	have given
see	saw	have seen
take	took	have taken
wear	wore	have worn
write	wrote	have written

1. Sentence 5: **Surprisingly, Uncle Joe say that he understood and that he supported my decision.**

    Which correction should be made to sentence 5?

    (1) change <u>say</u> to <u>said</u>
    (2) replace <u>say</u> with <u>told</u>
    (3) change <u>understood</u> to <u>understands</u>
    (4) change <u>supported</u> to <u>supports</u>
    (5) no correction is necessary

UNIT 4

Directions: Choose the <u>one best answer</u> to each question.

<u>Questions 2 and 3</u> refer to the following letter.

To Principal Johnson,

　(1) I have write down several reasons why the dress code the school board has recently proposed is a bad idea. (2) I wear different clothes to school, and I have never needed a dress code to tell me what's appropriate. (3) A dress code limits your ability to tell other people about your interests, opinions, and ideas. (4) It is also an easy way for school officials to get rid of ideas they don't like.

2. Sentence 1: **I have write down several reasons why the dress code the school board has recently proposed is a bad idea.**

   Which correction should be made to sentence 1?

   (1) replace <u>I</u> with <u>We</u>
   (2) replace <u>write</u> with <u>wrote</u>
   (3) change <u>have write</u> to <u>has written</u>
   (4) change <u>write</u> to <u>written</u>
   (5) no correction is necessary

3. Sentence 2: <u>**I wear different clothes to school,**</u> **and I have never needed a dress code to tell me what's appropriate.**

   Which is the best way to write the underlined portion of sentence 2? If the original is the best way, choose option (1).

   (1) I wear different clothes to school
   (2) I worn different clothes to school
   (3) I has worn different clothes to school
   (4) I have weared different clothes to school
   (5) I have worn different clothes to school

<u>Questions 4 and 5</u> refer to the following paragraph.

　(1) Have you recently tried to lose weight? (2) Maybe you have, but you also may gave up. (3) If so, Slim-A-Lot has a special offer for you. (4) We've spoken extensively on radio and TV about how delicious our frozen products are, and how they help you lose weight. (5) Now you can try them free for 30 days and have them bring straight to your home!

4. Sentence 2: **Maybe you have, <u>but you also may gave up</u>.**

   Which is the best way to write the underlined portion of sentence 2? If the original is the best way, choose option (1).

   (1) but you also may gave up
   (2) but you also may have given up
   (3) but you also are giving up
   (4) but you also give up
   (5) but you also gave up

5. Sentence 5: **Now you can try them free for 30 days <u>and have them bring straight to your home</u>!**

   Which is the best way to write the underlined portion of sentence 5? If the original is the best way, choose option (1).

   (1) and have them bring straight to your home
   (2) and have brought straight to your home
   (3) and have them brought straight to your home
   (4) and have brought them straight to your home
   (5) and had brought them straight to your home

Subject-Verb Agreement

① Learn the Skill

The subject and the verb are the most important parts of any sentence that you write. **Subject-verb agreement** makes sure that both parts of a sentence work well together. Verbs must agree with their subjects in number. The subject and the verb must be singular in a sentence, or they must be plural. Sometimes a sentence has two or more subjects that share the same verb. These subjects are called **compound subjects**. They take a plural verb regardless of the number of each part.

② Practice the Skill

By mastering the skill of using proper subject-verb agreement, you will improve your writing and test-taking skills, especially as they relate to the GED Language Arts/Writing Test. Read the paragraph and strategies below. Then answer the question that follows.

A In sentence 2, *Uncle Joe* is the singular subject, which means the writer uses the singular form of the verb *want*. *Uncle Joe wants* shows correct subject-verb agreement because it has a singular subject and a singular verb form.

B In sentence 5, *Uncle Joe and Aunt Mary* is a compound subject because it refers to two people. It takes the plural form of the verb *talk*. Compound subjects joined by *and* always take a plural verb: *Tom and Jan write*. When the parts of a compound subject are joined by *or*, the verb agrees with the part of the subject closest to the verb: *Tom or his friends write* in the park; *His friends or Tom writes* in the park.

(C)

(1) Mrs. Morgan be right, I need to say no and mean it. (2) **A** Uncle Joe wants me to move to Little Rock to work for him in his plumbing shop. (3) I say "No" to his requests, but he keeps pushing the issue. (4) I'm sure that he remembers the times that I tell him that I don't want to spend my vacations with him and Aunt Mary. (5) However, **B** Uncle Joe and Aunt Mary talk me into making the visit, and I have a great time. (6) I say "No" and then change my mind in response to Uncle Joe's requests. (7) He has no reason to think that this time is any different.

✓ TEST-TAKING TIPS

The following chart lists special singular and plural forms of the verbs *be, have,* and *do*. They do not follow the same forms as other verbs.

Verb	Singular	Plural
be	am, is, was	are, were
have	has	have
do	does	do

1. Sentence 1: **Mrs. Morgan be right, I need to say no and mean it.**

   Which is the best way to write the underlined portion of sentence 1? If the original is the best way, choose option (1).

   (1) Mrs. Morgan be right, I need to say no
   (2) Mrs. Morgan were right, I needed to say no
   (3) Mrs. Morgan am right, I need to say no
   (4) Mrs. Morgan is right, I need to say no
   (5) Mrs. Morgan are right, I needed to say no

Directions: Choose the <u>one best answer</u> to each question.

<u>Questions 2 and 3</u> refer to the following paragraph.

> (1) Thank you for purchasing your new cell phone. (2) Your new phones is also a radio transmitter and receiver. (3) It was designed and manufactured not to exceed certain limits set by the U.S. Government. (4) Scientists and phone technicians tests the phones frequently to make sure they are safe for everyone who will use them. (5) You will be getting more information about your new phone's safeguards in the mail within a few weeks.

2. Sentence 2: **Your new phones is also a radio transmitter and receiver.**

    Which correction should be made to sentence 2?

    (1) replace <u>Your</u> with <u>My</u>
    (2) change <u>is</u> to <u>be</u>
    (3) change <u>phones</u> to <u>phone</u>
    (4) replace <u>is</u> with <u>are</u>
    (5) no correction is necessary

3. Sentence 4: <u>**Scientists and phone technicians tests the phones**</u> **frequently to make sure they are safe for everyone who will use them.**

    Which is the best way to write the underlined portion of sentence 4? If the original is the best way, choose option (1).

    (1) Scientists and phone technicians tests the phones
    (2) Scientists and phone technicians test the phones
    (3) Scientists and phone technicians testing the phones
    (4) Scientist and phone technician testing the phones
    (5) Scientists and phone technicians will be test the phones

<u>Questions 4 and 5</u> refer to the following paragraph.

> (1) Office Supply's refund policies is simple. (2) If you paid with cash, Office Supply will refund your purchase with cash if it was bought at the same store. (3) If you paid with a debit card, we will credit your account the same day. (4) If you don't have your receipt, your return is only eligible for an in-store credit for the current price of the item you are returning. (5) Office Supply carefully monitor returns and, in some cases, returns without a receipt may be refused.

4. Sentence 1: **Office Supply's refund policies is simple.**

    Which correction should be made to sentence 1?

    (1) change <u>refund</u> to <u>refunds</u>
    (2) change <u>refund</u> to <u>refunding</u>
    (3) replace <u>is</u> with <u>are</u>
    (4) replace <u>is</u> with <u>was</u>
    (5) no correction is necessary

5. Sentence 5: **Office Supply carefully monitor returns and, in some cases, returns without a receipt may be refused.**

    Which correction should be made to sentence 5?

    (1) change <u>monitor</u> to <u>monitors</u>
    (2) change <u>Supply</u> to <u>supply</u>
    (3) replace <u>returns</u> with <u>return</u>
    (4) replace <u>a</u> with <u>the</u>
    (5) no correction is necessary

Subject-Verb Separation

usage
he
she
it
were
is

① Learn the Skill

Sometimes words and phrases separate a subject from its verb. **Subject-verb separation** is important to understand because the subject and verb must still agree even if they are separated. Phrases that might separate the subject and verb include those beginning with the words *together with*, *including*, *as well as*, *along with*, and *in addition to*. Subjects and verbs can also be inverted in sentences as well. This means that the verb appears in the sentence before the subject. However, the subject and verb must still agree no matter where they are located in a sentence.

② Practice the Skill

By mastering the skill of identifying subject-verb separation, you will improve your writing and test-taking skills, especially as they relate to the GED Language Arts/Writing Test. Read the paragraphs and strategies below. Then answer the question that follows.

A In sentence 3, the past tense singular verb *had* appears before the singular subject *I*. The inverted order makes the sentence sound different than the others in the passage, but it is correct because the subject and verb agree.

B In sentence 5, the singular subject *Uncle Joe* is separated from the verb *said* by the phrase *together with Aunt Mary*. Notice that the pronoun *he* is singular instead of plural. The words in the interrupting phrase are not part of the subject.

(D)

(1) It was time to put my thoughts into action. (2) At the end of the day, I dialed Uncle Joe's telephone number. (3) Never before <u>had I</u> been offered such an opportunity, I told him, but I had other plans. (4) I said that I knew he was probably disappointed, but I would not change my mind. (5) Surprisingly <u>Uncle Joe</u>, together with Aunt Mary, said that <u>he</u> understood and that <u>he</u> supported my decision.

(E)

(6) Although Mrs. Morgan's advice was simple, it was valuable. (7) She taught me the importance of matching my words with my thoughts. (8) By following this advice, I gained self-confidence. (9) Now I, in addition to choosing my words carefully, controls my own future. (10) I say what I mean, and I get what I want.

✓ TEST-TAKING TIPS

Omit the interrupting phrase as you read sentence 5 quietly to yourself: *Uncle Joe said.* Now you can be sure that the subject and verb agree. Use this technique with other sentences to ensure proper subject-verb agreement.

1. Sentence 9: **Now I, in addition to choosing my words carefully, controls my own future.**

   Which correction should be made to sentence 9?

   (1) remove the comma after <u>Now I</u>
   (2) replace <u>words</u> with <u>word</u>
   (3) move <u>carefully</u> to follow <u>choosing</u>
   (4) change <u>controls</u> to <u>control</u>
   (5) no correction is necessary

UNIT 4

Questions 2 and 3 refer to the following paragraph.

Directions: Choose the <u>one best answer</u> to each question.

> (1) There is a simple way to get the best price on a new car. (2) This simple, 3-step system can save thousands of dollars on your next car. (3) Step 1 is to find out what the dealer has paid for the car. (4) Step 2, in addition to step 1, are to ask whether the dealer has received a hidden rebate for the car. (5) Dealer, by the end of last year, receive all kinds of rebates from car makers. (6) They will try to keep these rebates hidden from you during the deal! (7) Step 3 is to ask the dealer what his employees pay for a car. (8) Knowing these things, can you bargain with any dealer? (9) The answer is yes!

2. Sentence 4: **Step 2, in addition to step 1, are to ask whether the dealer has received a hidden rebate for the car.**

   Which correction should be made to sentence 4?

   (1) change <u>dealer</u> to <u>dealers</u>
   (2) replace <u>are</u> with <u>be</u>
   (3) replace <u>are</u> with <u>is</u>
   (4) replace <u>in addition to</u> with <u>on the other hand</u>
   (5) no correction is necessary

3. Sentence 5: <u>**Dealer, by the end of last year, receive** all kinds of rebates from car makers.</u>

   Which is the best way to write the underlined portion of sentence 5? If the original is the best way, choose option (1).

   (1) Dealer, by the end of last year, receive
   (2) Dealer at the end of the year received
   (3) Dealers last year receives
   (4) Dealers, by the end of last year, had received
   (5) A dealer receive at the end of the year

Questions 4 and 5 refer to the following paragraph.

> (1) Have you ever gone apple picking? (2) Apple, the ones in an apple orchard, does not begin to ripen until early fall. (3) Different kinds of apples ripen at different times. (4) Some of the first to ripen are McIntosh apples. (5) They have a sweet, in addition to a tart, tastes. (6) On the other hand, Fuji apples are some of the last to ripen. (7) They tend to be crisp and sweet. (8) If you pick apples before they are ripe, they may not taste good. (9) Waiting until fall to pick apples is a good idea, even if they start appearing in the apple orchard in late summer.

4. Sentence 2: <u>**Apple, the ones in an apple orchard, does not begin**</u> to ripen until early fall.

   Which is the best way to write the underlined portion of sentence 2? If the original is the best way, choose option (1).

   (1) Apple, the ones in an apple orchard, does not begin
   (2) Apples in an apple orchard does not begin
   (3) Apple, the ones in an apple orchard, do not begin
   (4) Apples in an orchard does not begin
   (5) Apples, the ones in an apple orchard, do not begin

5. Sentence 5: **They have a sweet, in addition to a tart, tastes.**

   Which correction should be made to sentence 5?

   (1) change <u>tastes</u> to <u>taste</u>
   (2) replace <u>in addition to</u> with <u>however</u>
   (3) replace <u>They</u> with <u>McIntosh apples</u>
   (4) replace <u>They</u> with <u>Them</u>
   (5) no correction is necessary

Unit 4 Review

The Unit Review is structured to resemble the GED Language Arts/Writing Test. Be sure to read each question and all possible answers very carefully before choosing your answer.

To record your answers, fill in the numbered circle that corresponds to the answer you select for each question in the Unit Review.

Do not rest your pencil on the answer area while considering your answer. Make no stray or unnecessary marks. If you change an answer, erase your first mark completely.

Mark only one answer space for each question; multiple answers will be scored as incorrect.

Sample Question

Sentence 8: **It's not just my neighborhood, either.**

Which of the following words from sentence 8 is a noun?

(1) It's
(2) just
(3) my
(4) neighborhood
(5) either

Directions: Choose the <u>one best answer</u> to each question.

<u>Questions 1 through 6</u> refer to the following letter.

To Whom It May Concern,

(A)

(1) As an animal lover, I am sad to see how many stray and abandoned cats are living in my neighborhood. (2) Many of them is about to have kittens, while others seem to be wild. (3) Cats are even living in abandoned houses. (4) It's sad to see these poor animals that have no one to care for them.

(B)

(5) I care about cats, but there is only so much that I can do for cats. (6) I asked the local dog officer to come to my neighborhood. (7) She looked at a pregnant cat and made sure it was seen by a veterinarian.

(C)

(8) It's not just my neighborhood, either. (9) There is much abandoned cat in every neighborhood in the city. (10) Pet owner need to be responsible and not let their animal go outside without being spayed or neutered.

Sincerely,

Jenny Briggs

1. Sentence 2: **Many of them is about to have kittens**, while others seem to be wild.

Which is the best way to write the underlined portion of sentence 2? If the original is the best way, choose option (1).

(1) Many of them is about to have kittens
(2) Many about to have kittens
(3) Many of them are about to have kittens
(4) Many of them were about to have kittens
(5) Many of them are kittens

①②③④⑤

2. Sentence 4: **It's sad to see these poor animals that have no one to care for them.**

Which of the following words from sentence 4 is a noun?

(1) It's
(2) animals
(3) see
(4) have
(5) them

①②③④⑤

3. Sentence 5: **I care about cats, but there is only so much that I can do for cats.**

Which is the best way to write the underlined portion of sentence 5? If the original is the best way, choose option (1).

(1) is only so much that I can do for cats
(2) was only so much I can do for cats
(3) is only so much they could do for me
(4) is only so much I can do for them
(5) is only so much we can do for it

①②③④⑤

4. Sentence 7: **She looked at a pregnant cat and made sure it was seen by a veterinarian.**

Which correction should be made to sentence 7?

(1) replace looked with looks
(2) change She to Her
(3) replace cat with animal
(4) change made to makes
(5) no correction is necessary

①②③④⑤

5. Sentence 9: **There is much abandoned cat in every neighborhood in the city.**

Which is the best way to write the underlined portion of sentence 9? If the original is the best way, choose option (1).

(1) There is much abandoned cat in every
(2) There is many abandoned cats in every
(3) There are much abandoned cats in every
(4) There are many abandoned cats in every
(5) There are many an abandoned cat in every

①②③④⑤

6. Sentence 10: **Pet owner need to be responsible and not let their animal go outside without being spayed or neutered.**

Which is the best way to write the underlined portion of sentence 10? If the original is the best way, choose option (1).

(1) Pet owner need to be responsible and not let their animal go
(2) Pet owners need to be responsible and not let their animal goes
(3) Pet owner need to be responsible and not let their animals goes
(4) Pet owner needed to be responsible and not let their animals go
(5) Pet owners need to be responsible and not let their animals go

①②③④⑤

Directions: Choose the <u>one best answer</u> to each question.

Questions 7 through 12 refer to the following information.

EZ Phone Instructions

(A)

(1) Your new EZ Phone is simple and wireless. (2) You simply pay as you go. (3) With EZ Phone, you buy the phone and prepay for your minutes by buying EZ Phone Airtime cards. (4) Your phone keeps track of how much airtime you used and how much are left. (5) It displays the airtime balance on your phone, so that you can control how much your will be. (6) The minutes you buy for your EZ Phone are referred to as "units." (7) One minute of a local or long distance call is equal to one unit of airtime. (8) If someone calls you and you be outside of your home area, one minute of call time will equal two units of airtime. (9) Reading or sending a text message takes one half of one unit.

(B)

(10) To make or receive a call on your EZ Phone, you must has units left in your balance. (11) You must also have a due date that has not passed, even if units you have remaining. (12) To keep your EZ Phone service working, you must buy and add a new group of unit before the due date. (13) Otherwise, you will lose your phone number and your service.

---

7. Sentence 4: **Your phone keeps track of how much airtime you used and how much are left**.

Which is the best way to write the underlined portion of sentence 4? If the original is the best way, choose option (1).

(1) how much airtime you used and how much are left
(2) how much airtime you use and how much is left
(3) how much airtime you have used and how much be left
(4) how much airtime you used and how much was left
(5) how much airtime you are using and how much will be left

① ② ③ ④ ⑤

8. Sentence 5: **It displays the airtime balance on the phone, so that you can control how much your will be.**

Which correction should be made to sentence 5?

(1) insert a noun after your
(2) insert a comma before will
(3) insert a verb after your
(4) insert a pronoun before will
(5) no correction is necessary

① ② ③ ④ ⑤

9. Sentence 8: **If someone calls you and you be outside of your home area, one minute of call time will equal two units of airtime.**

Which correction should be made to sentence 8?

(1) change calls to called
(2) replace be with is
(3) change will equal to equaled
(4) replace be with are
(5) no correction is necessary

① ② ③ ④ ⑤

10. Sentence 10: **To make or receive a call on your EZ Phone, you must has units left in your balance.**

Which correction should be made to sentence 10?

(1) replace receive with received
(2) change has to had
(3) replace your with my
(4) change has to have
(5) no correction is necessary

① ② ③ ④ ⑤

11. Sentence 11: **You must also have a due date that has not passed, even if units you have remaining**.

Which is the best way to write the underlined portion of sentence 11? If the original is the best way, choose option (1).

(1) even if units you have remaining
(2) even if your units are remaining
(3) even if you have units remaining
(4) even the units you have remain
(5) even if you had units remaining

① ② ③ ④ ⑤

12. Sentence 12: **To keep your EZ Phone service working, you must buy and add a new group of unit before the due date.**

Which correction should be made to sentence 12?

(1) replace Phone with phone
(2) remove the comma after working
(3) change you to I
(4) change unit to units
(5) no correction is necessary

① ② ③ ④ ⑤

Directions: Choose the <u>one best answer</u> to each question.

<u>Questions 13 through 18</u> refer to the following information.

Summons for Jury Duty: Nebraska

(A)

(1) After the witnesses finish their testimony, the judge will instruct you about the law regarding the case. (2) You must base your decision-making on the judge's instructions about the law instead of your own ideas about what the law is or should be. (3) You and other members of the jury will be taken to the jury room. (4) One jury member will be selected as the foreperson. (5) They will lead your discussions and bring your verdict into court.

(B)

(6) Your discussions in the jury room should include an honest expression of your opinions. (7) Your discussions should also be tolerant and respectful of other people's opinions. (8) In a civil case, you may have to decide if there is any reason to pay damages, and if so how much. (9) If the jury cannot reach a unanimous verdict in a civil case within six hours, then a decision reached by 10 members of a 12-person jury is acceptable.

(C)

(10) In a criminal case, jury discussions is done when a unanimous verdict has been reached. (11) If the juries, after long discussions, cannot reach a verdict, the foreperson must tell the judge. (12) The jury have nothing to do with sentencing if it returns a guilty verdict.

---

13. Sentence 2: **You must base your decision-making on the judge's instructions about the law <u>instead of your own ideas about what the law is or should be</u>.**

Which is the best way to write the underlined portion of sentence 2? If the original is the best way, choose option (1).

(1) instead of your own ideas about what the law is or should be
(2) instead of you idea about what the law should be or is
(3) rather than your idea of laws
(4) instead of what your ideals are
(5) rather than your own ideas about laws

①②③④⑤

14. Sentence 5: **They will lead your discussions and bring your verdict into court.**

Which correction should be made to sentence 5?

(1) change <u>They</u> to <u>The foreperson</u>
(2) replace <u>discussions</u> with <u>discussion</u>
(3) change <u>They</u> to <u>He</u>
(4) insert a comma after <u>discussions</u>
(5) no correction is necessary

①②③④⑤

15. Sentence 7: **Your discussions should also be tolerant and respectful of other people's opinions.**

Which correction should be made to sentence 7?

(1) replace <u>also be</u> with <u>be also</u>
(2) replace <u>be</u> with <u>are</u>
(3) replace <u>opinions</u> with <u>opinion</u>
(4) remove <u>people's</u>
(5) no correction is necessary

①②③④⑤

16. Sentence 10: **In a criminal case, <u>jury discussions is done when a unanimous verdict has been reached</u>.**

Which is the best way to write the underlined portion of sentence 10? If the original is the best way, choose option (1).

(1) jury discussions is done when a unanimous verdict has been reached
(2) jury discussions are done when a unanimous verdict has been reached
(3) jury discussions were done when a unanimous verdict has been reached
(4) jury discussions are done when a unanimous verdict have been reached
(5) jury discussions are done when a unanimous verdict was been reached

①②③④⑤

17. Sentence 11: **If the juries, after long discussions, cannot reach a verdict, the foreperson must tell the judge.**

Which correction should be made to sentence 11?

(1) replace <u>juries</u> with <u>jury</u>
(2) replace <u>the foreperson</u> with <u>they</u>
(3) remove the comma after <u>discussions</u>
(4) replace <u>judge</u> with <u>Judge</u>
(5) no correction is necessary

①②③④⑤

18. Sentence 12: **The <u>jury have nothing to do with sentencing</u> if it returns a guilty verdict.**

Which is the best way to write the underlined portion of sentence 12? If the original is the best way, choose option (1).

(1) jury have nothing to do with sentencing
(2) jury has nothing to does with sentencing
(3) jury has nothing to do with sentencing
(4) jury has not to do with sentences
(5) juries have nothing to do with sentences

①②③④⑤

WALTER ANDERSON

Anderson earned his GED certificate while enlisted in the Marines and has since become a publishing icon.

Walter Anderson found storybook success in magazines. However, his childhood was anything but. Born in Mount Vernon, New York, Anderson spent much of his childhood being punished by his father for reading books. Fortunately, his mother encouraged him to read, regardless of the consequences. Anderson later asked his mother why she encouraged him to read despite the fact that his father would punish him for it. She responded,

> **❝I knew that if you would learn to read, somehow you would find your way out, and you have.❞**

Anderson believes his mother's faith in him was a key ingredient in his success. He was a bright child, finishing both eighth and ninth grade in one school year. Unfortunately, he had a difficult time finding his place and left high school without graduating. Anderson then joined the U.S. Marines in 1961. While enlisted, he earned his GED certificate. After leaving the military, he enrolled in college to become a writer and editor.

Anderson served as the editor of *PARADE* for 20 years, during which time he increased the magazine's circulation from 21.6 million in 129 Sunday newspapers to 37 million in 340 newspapers. Anderson became Chairman, Publisher, and CEO of Parade Publications in February 2000.

Anderson has been a national spokesperson for the GED Tests, as well as the director of the Dropout Prevention Fund. Among the many honors he has received, he is particularly proud of the Horatio Alger Award he received in 1994. The award is given to individuals who have achieved success despite difficult childhoods.

BIO BLAST: *Walter Anderson*

- Born in Mount Vernon, New York
- Joined prestigious group that includes Maya Angelou, Colin Powell, and Oprah Winfrey by earning Horatio Alger Award in 1994
- Has written several books, including *The Confidence Course* and *Courage is a Three-Letter Word*
- Wrote *Meant to Be* in which he chronicled the emotional and physical abuse he endured from his father

Unit 5: Mechanics

Spelling and punctuation are the nuts and bolts of sentences. When you write, words and punctuation marks work together to express an idea. In Unit 5, you will learn the mechanics of the English language, such as spelling and capitalization. Take a moment to familiarize yourself with the following glossary of terms, noting the examples provided. These terms will appear throughout the book.

GLOSSARY OF TERMS

Proper adjective: A proper noun, or a word that begins with a capital letter but does not necessarily begin a sentence, that describes another noun: _English_ books, _Thanksgiving_ dinner.

Quotations: Exact speech which is preceded and immediately followed by quotation marks: _"Cortland apples are my favorite,"_ John said.

Homophones and Homographs: Homophones are words that sound similar but have different spellings and different meanings: _acts_ are deeds; an _ax_ is a tool. Homographs are words that have the same spelling but different meanings: a _bat_ is both a flying animal and a stick for hitting a ball.

Pronunciation: The way a word is spoken.

Introductory word/phrase: Words or phrases that introduce a main clause: _Finally, the movie was released_; _After the movie, we went to dinner_.

Interrupting phrase: A group of words immediately preceded and followed by commas, and which interrupt a main clause: _Apple season, which starts in the fall, is a wonderful time for picnics_.

Vowel: The letters _a, e, i, o, u_, and sometimes _y_.

Semicolon: A punctuation mark (;) used between independent clauses without coordinating conjunctions, independent clauses linked by conjunctive adverbs, and items in a series that contains other punctuation.

Colon: A punctuation mark (:) used to separate clauses and to begin lists or examples.

Hyphen: Punctuation that is used to join two-word modifiers: _Her hair is reddish-blonde_.

Dash: En dashes are used mostly to show ranges: He ran _10–15_ yards. Em dashes are generally used to separate information within sentences: _This magazine—started by two college students—was founded in 1987_.

Parentheses: Punctuation that is used to isolate information relating to the main clause, but could be omitted: _The bridges (especially the long ones) are dangerous during the winter_.

Table of Contents

Capitalization

Mechanics

A _____

" _____ .

" _____ "

1 Learn the Skill

Standardized rules regarding written language help writers communicate effectively with an audience. The rules are intended to help writers clearly and effectively convey ideas through writing. Keeping this idea in mind, let's review the rules for **capitalization**. Writers must use capital letters to identify proper nouns (*Bent Pine Drive*), proper adjectives (*United States government*), titles (*Ms., Dr.*), holidays (*Thanksgiving*), days of the week (*Saturday*), and months of the year (*April*). Writers should also use a capital letter to signal the beginning of a sentence and the beginning of a direct quotation. Additionally, the word *I* is always capitalized.

2 Practice the Skill

By mastering the skill of capitalization, you will improve your writing and test-taking skills, especially as they relate to the GED Language Arts/Writing Test. Read the paragraph and strategies below. Then answer the question that follows.

A Notice that this paragraph does not contain capital letters. Identify each title, each proper noun, words that begin sentences or quotations, and each instance of the word *I*.

B Capitalization is important because it indicates the proper nouns and other words of importance. For example, *little rock* and *Little Rock*. If it is not clear that the writer is referring to a city, the reader could think the writer is simply talking about a small rock.

☑ **TEST-TAKING TIPS**

When reading a paragraph with capitalization errors, draw three small lines under any letter that should be capitalized: <u>little</u> <u>rock</u>. This standard editing notation will help you answer capitalization questions.

(C)
(1) **A** <u>mrs. morgan</u> was right; i needed to say no and mean it. (2) uncle joe wanted me to move to **B** <u>little rock</u> to work for him in his plumbing shop. (3) i had said "no" to his previous requests, but he kept pushing the issue. (4) i'm sure he remembered the time i told him i didn't want to spend three weeks with him and aunt mary during my vacation. (5) however, i had let my uncle talk me into making the visit, and i ended up having a great time. (6) i'd said "no" and then changed my mind a dozen times in response to uncle joe's requests. (7) he had no reason to think that this time would be any different.

1. Sentence 2: **uncle joe wanted me to move to little rock to work for him in his plumbing shop.**

   Which corrections should be made to sentence 2?

   (1) capitalize *joe, him, move, plumbing,* and *shop*
   (2) capitalize *uncle, joe, little,* and *rock*
   (3) capitalize *uncle, little, rock, him,* and *move*
   (4) capitalize *little, rock, him, move,* and *plumbing*
   (5) no corrections are necessary

Directions: Choose the <u>one best answer</u> to each question.

<u>Questions 2 through 4</u> refer to the following information.

Paying Bills Online

(A)

(1) How often do you pay bills each month? (2) You probably pay bills twice per month—around the first and fifteenth of january, for example. (3) How much time do you spend writing checks and addressing and stamping envelopes? (4) If you spend an hour per session, that's two hours per month. (5) Over the course of a year, you might spend 24 hours paying bills. (6) That's a whole day!

(B)

(7) In addition, if you pay 20 bills per month, you are spending additional money on postage. (8) At 41 cents per letter, you spend more than $8.00 per month or close to $100 per year on postage alone. (9) Does it make sense that you're paying money to the United States Postal Service to take your money to your creditors? (10) Of course not, when I put it that way, right?

(C)

(11) There are several advantages to online banking. (12) For one, you'll get that day back each year. (13) Additionally, you'll save the money you're spending on postage. (14) You will also save any money you're spending on late fees because many online banking services provide you with real-time alerts.

(D)

(15) Another advantage of online banking is a paperless lifestyle. (16) You'll save pine trees, and You'll reduce clutter in your home. (17) You will no longer need a filing system for cancelled checks, banking statements, or billing statements. (18) Yet, all of this information will be easily accessible to you whenever you need it via a computer.

---

2. Sentence 2: **You probably pay bills twice per month—around the first and fifteenth of january, for example.**

   Which correction should be made to sentence 2?

   (1) replace <u>january</u> with <u>January</u>
   (2) replace the comma with a semicolon
   (3) replace <u>around</u> with <u>Around</u>
   (4) remove <u>for example</u>
   (5) no correction is necessary

3. Sentence 9: **Does it make sense that you're paying money to the United States Postal Service to pay money to your creditors?**

   Why is United States Postal Service capitalized?

   (1) It is the beginning of a sentence.
   (2) It is a day of the week.
   (3) It is a proper noun.
   (4) It is a person's title.
   (5) It is a holiday.

4. Sentence 16: **You'll save <u>pine trees, and You'll reduce</u> clutter in your home.**

   Which is the best way to write the underlined portion of sentence 16? If the original is the best way, choose option (1).

   (1) pine trees, and You'll reduce
   (2) pine trees; and You'll reduce
   (3) Pine Trees, and you'll reduce
   (4) pine trees, and you'll reduce
   (5) Pine Trees And You'll Reduce

Possessives and Contractions

① Learn the Skill

When writing, you may need to indicate possession or ownership. Use an apostrophe to create a **possessive**: *Shelley's book* or *Willis's computer*. You may also want to use **contractions**, which are created by combining words and using an apostrophe to indicate that one or more letters or numbers have been removed: *won't (will not), can't (cannot), I'm (I am),* and *'68 (1968)*. Generally, contractions are used in informal writing or dialogue as a way to imitate speech.

② Practice the Skill

By mastering the skill of using possessives and contractions, you will improve your writing and test-taking skills, especially as they relate to the GED Language Arts/Writing Test. Read the paragraph and strategies below. Then answer the question that follows.

A Sentence 6 contains two contractions: *don't* and *they'll*. *Don't* is a combination of the words *do not*, and *they'll* is a combination of *they will*.

B Sentence 8 contains a common singular possessive: *Mrs. Morgan's*. A singular possessive results in an *'s* being added, even if the word ends in an *s: Silas's boat.* Other examples include a plural word without an *s: children = children's;* a plural word with an *s: musicians = musicians'.* A compound word: *mother-in-law = mother-in-law's* and a co-possession: *Emily and Anna = Emily and Anna's.*

(A)
(1) "When you say no, mean it," Mrs. Morgan, my former U.S. History teacher, laughed, as she brushed a strand of reddish-blond hair from her eyes. (2) We were standing together in the hallway outside one wing of my old school. (3) The warm afternoon sun kept us from other obligations. (4) "That's one thing I always tried to do with my children. (5) I didn't want to send the message that I didn't mean what I said. (6) If people think you <u>don't</u> mean what you say, <u>they'll</u> take advantage of you," she finished, giving me a motherly look. (7) "Don't change you're mind often," she added. (8) Although I didn't know it at the time, <u>Mrs. Morgan's</u> advice would change my life in a positive way.

☑ TEST-TAKING TIPS

To determine whether a possessive is necessary, rephrase the sentence with *of the: the girl's doll = the doll of the girl.* Beware of tricky contractions and possessives: *it's* (contraction of *it is*) and *its* (possessive pronoun); *you're* (contraction of *you are*) and *your* (possessive pronoun; and *they're* (contraction of *they are*) and *their* (possessive pronoun).

1. Sentence 7: **"Don't change you're mind often,"**
   she added.

   Which correction should be made to sentence 7?

   (1) replace <u>Don't</u> with <u>Dont</u>
   (2) change <u>you're</u> to <u>your</u>
   (3) replace <u>added</u> with <u>adding</u>
   (4) change <u>she</u> to <u>She</u>
   (5) no correction is necessary

Directions: Choose the <u>one best answer</u> to each question.

<u>Questions 2 through 4</u> refer to the following information.

**Community Bulletin
Tornado Preparedness**

**(A)
BEFORE A TORNADO**

- (1) Choose a safe meeting place away from windows' such as a basement, bathroom, or hallway.
- (2) Prepare a disaster kit that includes the following items: a first aid kit, food, water, clothes, bedding, a radio, flashlights, and extra batteries.
- (3) Store the disaster kit in the safe meeting place.

**(B)
DURING A TORNADO WATCH**

- (4) Stay tuned to a local radio or television station.
- (5) Use you're senses. (6) If you see blowing objects or hear a train-like sound, go to a designated safe meeting place.

**(C)
DURING A TORNADO WARNING**

- (7) Immediately go to a designated safe meeting place.
- (8) Retrieve the familys disaster kit.

**(D)
AFTER A TORNADO**

- (9) Stay tuned to a local radio or television station for guidance.
- (10) Avoid damaged areas.

---

2. Sentence 1: **Choose a safe meeting place away from windows' such as a basement, bathroom, or hallway.**

   Which correction should be made to sentence 1?

   (1) replace the apostrophe after <u>windows</u> with a comma
   (2) replace <u>such as</u> with <u>for example</u>
   (3) change <u>basement</u> to <u>basement's</u>
   (4) remove the comma after <u>bathroom</u>
   (5) no correction is necessary

3. Sentences 5 and 6: **Use you're senses. If you see blowing objects or hear a train-like sound, go to a designated safe meeting place.**

   Which correction should be made to sentences 5 and 6?

   (1) replace <u>senses. If</u> with <u>senses, however</u>
   (2) remove the comma after <u>sound</u>
   (3) change <u>senses.</u> to <u>senses;</u>
   (4) replace <u>you're</u> with <u>your</u>
   (5) no correction is necessary

4. Sentence 8: **Retrieve the familys disaster kit.**

   Which correction should be made to sentence 8?

   (1) replace <u>familys</u> with <u>family's</u>
   (2) change <u>familys</u> to <u>familys'</u>
   (3) change <u>kit</u> to <u>kit's</u>
   (4) remove <u>familys</u>
   (5) no correction is necessary

UNIT 5

Homonyms

Mechanics

A_____
"_____.
_____
"

① Learn the Skill

Homophones are words that sound similar when spoken aloud, but they have different spellings and different meanings. For example, *acts* are deeds, and an *ax* is a tool. **Homographs** are words that have the same spellings but different meanings. For example, a *bat* is both a flying animal and a stick for hitting a ball. Homographs may have the same pronunciations, or the pronunciations may be varied. Both types of words can be called **homonyms**.

② Practice the Skill

By mastering the skill of using homonyms correctly, you will improve your writing and test-taking skills, especially as they relate to the GED Language Arts/Writing Test. Read the paragraph and strategies below. Then answer the question that follows.

A *To* is a homophone because it sounds the same as *two* (the number) and *too* (also; in excess). Other homophone pairings include *for*: *four* and *their*: *there*.

B *Too* is also a homograph because it has two meanings: also (*I am going, too*) and in excess (*There are too many people going*).

C Note that in addition to being possessives and contractions, the words *its* and *it's*, *your* and *you're*, and *their* and *they're* are homophones.

(C)

(1) Mrs. Morgan was right; I needed <u>to</u> say no and mean it. (2) Uncle Joe wanted me to move to Little Rock to work for him in his plumbing shop. (3) I had said "No" to his previous requests, but he kept pushing the issue. (4) I'm sure he remembered the time I told him I didn't want to spend three weeks with him and Aunt Mary during my vacation. (5) However, I let my uncle talk me into making the visit, and I ended up having a great time. (6) I know I've said "No" <u>too</u> many times and then changed my mind in response to Uncle Joe's requests. (7) He had no reason to think that this time would be any different. (8) But Aunt Mary and Uncle Joe understood because <u>they're</u> reasonable, understanding people.

✓ **TEST-TAKING TIPS**

Carefully examine the words or phrases that surround a homophone or homograph to determine which homonym a writer intends.

1. Sentence 6: **I know I've said "No" too many times and then changed my mind in response to Uncle Joe's requests.**

Which of the following words from sentence 6 is part of a homophone pairing?

(1) no: know
(2) mind: mine
(3) then: than
(4) times: tines
(5) said: red

Directions: Choose the <u>one best answer</u> to each question.

<u>Questions 2 through 4</u> refer to the following information.

Putting the Brakes on Bad Habits

(A)

(1) Everyone has a bad habit or two. (2) Whatever the guilty obsession may be, you know that you shouldn't be doing it. (3) Yet, you continue to find time (or make time) for this habit in your busy schedule. (4) So, if knowing the behavior is bad for you doesn't help you brake it, what will?

(B)

(5) Won strategy that helps someone break a bad habit is to stop spending time with a clique that engages in the same habit. (6) If others enable your bad habits, stop spending time with them. (7) Find people who engage in good habits.

(C)

(8) Another strategy that helps someone break a bad habit is taking control of one's schedule. (9) Use any flexibility that you have within your work schedule to plan for good habits. (10) If you have only a few minutes for lunch, pack a healthy lunch rather than jetting out to the nearest fast-food drive-through lane. (11) If you normally bite your nails, put on a clear coat of nail polish. (12) If you have a ten-minute morning coffee break, ask a friend to join you in walking a couple of times around the boarder of the parking lot. (13) By taking control of these flexible moments within your day, you'll begin to take control of your habits, too.

---

2. Sentence 4: **So, if knowing the behavior is bad for you doesn't help you brake it, what will?**

   Which correction should be made to sentence 4?

   (1) replace <u>knowing</u> with <u>no</u>
   (2) insert a period after <u>will</u>
   (3) change <u>for</u> to <u>four</u>
   (4) replace <u>brake</u> with <u>break</u>
   (5) no correction is necessary

3. Sentence 5: **Won strategy that helps someone break a bad habit is to stop spending time with a clique that engages in the same habit.**

   Which correction should be made to sentence 5?

   (1) replace <u>clique</u> with <u>click</u>
   (2) replace <u>to</u> with <u>too</u>
   (3) replace <u>Won</u> with <u>One</u>
   (4) replace <u>time</u> with <u>thyme</u>
   (5) no correction is necessary

4. Sentence 12: **If you have a ten-minute morning coffee break, ask a friend to join you in walking a couple of times around the boarder of the parking lot.**

   Which correction should be made to sentence 12?

   (1) replace <u>ten</u> with <u>tin</u>
   (2) change <u>break</u> to <u>brake</u>
   (3) replace <u>boarder</u> with <u>border</u>
   (4) change <u>have</u> to <u>had</u>
   (5) no correction is necessary

Commonly Misspelled Words

1 Learn the Skill

Standardized spelling makes written communication possible because writers and readers agree that a particular combination of letters represents a particular word. While there are rules that preside over the spelling of some words, such as *i* before *e* except after *c*, other words defy such rules, such as *science*. There are several hundred commonly used English words that contain tricky spelling patterns because they do not follow any rules or are not spelled the way they sound. These **commonly misspelled words** must be memorized.

2 Practice the Skill

By mastering the skill of correctly spelling commonly misspelled words, you will improve your writing and test-taking skills, especially as they relate to the GED Language Arts/Writing Test. Read the paragraph and strategies below. Then answer the question that follows.

A *February* is commonly misspelled because people often forget about the first *r: Febuary* is not correct.

B Other commonly misspelled words include:

acknowledgment	hesitate
beneficial	independent
column	knowledge
conscientious	library
explanation	mischievous
guarantee	surprisingly

(D)

(1) It was time to put my thoughts into action. (2) At the end of a long day in <u>February</u>, I dialed Uncle Joe's telephone number. (3) I told him that I apreciated the offer of work, but I had other plans. (4) I said that I knew he was probably disappointed, but I would not change my mind. (5) <u>Surprisingly</u>, Uncle Joe said he understood and that he supported my <u>decision</u>.

✎ WRITING STRATEGIES

Identify words you frequently misspell. Look at the word spelled correctly. Touch each letter with the tip of a pencil, and say the letter aloud. Repeat this process five times. Then cover the word and write it from memory. Repeat this process until you've mastered the spelling.

1. Sentence 3: **I told him that I apreciated the offer of work, but I had other plans.**

   Which correction should be made to sentence 3?

   (1) change <u>of</u> to <u>off</u>
   (2) replace <u>offer</u> with <u>offur</u>
   (3) change <u>apreciated</u> to <u>appreciated</u>
   (4) replace <u>work</u> with <u>wurk</u>
   (5) no correction is necessary

③ Apply the Skill

Directions: Choose the <u>one best answer</u> to each question.

<u>Questions 2 through 4</u> refer to the following information.

**Press Release
Research Laboratories, Inc.**

(A)

(1) The soybean has long been popular in the diets of Asians and vegetarians, who consume soybeans in the forms of sauce, meal, oil, and milk. (2) Soybeans are also used to produce tofu or bean curd and miso or soybean paste. (3) In addition to its nutritional value as an alternative protein, the soybean is used in the production of soaps, paints, plastics, and inks. (4) Additionally, the soybean is relatively easy to grow and harvest. (5) Soybeans are grown in the United States and South America. (6) China and Japan import great quantities of soybeans.

(B)

(7) Research conducted in our labratories suggests that the consumption of soybeans is benaficial for human health. (8) Soy protein has been shown to decrease bad cholesterol and increase good cholesterol. (9) This result contributes to heart health.

(C)

(10) Chemicals in soybeans have been shown to promote bone health and reduce the risk of osteoporosis. (11) In addition, soybeans contain calcium, magnesium, and boron, which also contribute to healthy bones. (12) Also, soy products may help reduce menopausal symptoms such as hot flashes and night sweats.

(D)

(13) Finally, soy products may help prevent or treat prostate cancer. (14) Our scientists are engaged in ongoing research regarding the relationship between soy and breast cancer. (15) It is our hope that this research will put to rest the contraversy surrounding soy and breast cancer.

---

2. Sentence 7: **Research conducted in our <u>labratories suggests that the consumption of soybeans is benaficial</u> for human health.**

   Which is the best way to write the underlined portion of sentence 7? If the original is the best way, choose option (1).

   (1) labratories suggests that the consumption of soybeans is benaficial
   (2) laboratories suggests that the consumption of soybeans is beneficial
   (3) laboratories suggest that the consumption of soybeans is beneficial
   (4) laboratorys suggests that the consumption of soybeans is benefishal
   (5) laboratory suggests that the consumption of soybeans is benuficial

3. Sentence 10: **Chemicals in soybeans have been shown to promote bone health and reduce the risk of osteoporosis.**

   Which correction should be made to sentence 10?

   (1) change <u>soybeans</u> to <u>soy beans</u>
   (2) replace <u>promote</u> with <u>premote</u>
   (3) change <u>health</u> to <u>heallth</u>
   (4) replace <u>risk</u> with <u>risque</u>
   (5) no correction is necessary

4. Sentence 15: **It is our hope that this research will put to rest the contraversy surrounding soy and breast cancer.**

   Which correction should be made to sentence 15?

   (1) change <u>our</u> to <u>are</u>
   (2) replace <u>contraversy</u> with <u>controversy</u>
   (3) change <u>surrounding</u> to <u>surounding</u>
   (4) replace <u>soy</u> with <u>soye</u>
   (5) no correction is necessary

Commas

① Learn the Skill

A **comma** separates words into meaningful units within a sentence. Commas help writers express their ideas, and they help readers understand the meaning of a text. Review the comma rules cited below to improve your reading and writing skills.

② Practice the Skill

By mastering the skill of comma placement, you will improve your writing and test-taking skills, especially as they relate to the GED Language Arts/Writing Test. Read the paragraph and strategies below. Then answer the questions that follow.

Ⓐ Commas can be used in:
- **Introductory words/phrases:** Now, I control my own future by choosing my words carefully.
- **interrupting phrases:** Mrs. Morgan, my former teacher, gave me some simple but valuable advice.
- **quotations (dialogue):** I say, "Get what you want by saying what you mean."

(E)
(1) **Ⓐ** <u>Although Mrs. Morgan's advice was simple,</u> it was valuable. (2) She taught me the importance of matching my words with my thoughts. (3) By following this advice I gained **Ⓑ** <u>self-confidence, self-esteem, and self-control.</u> (4) Now, I control my own future by choosing my words carefully. (5) I say what I mean, and I get what I want.

Ⓑ Use commas to create:
- **a series:** self-confidence, self-esteem, and self-control
- **compound sentences:** I say what I mean, and I get what I want.
- **complex sentences:** Although Mrs. Morgan's advice was simple, it was valuable.

☑ TEST-TAKING TIPS

To determine when a comma should be used, read a sentence aloud, or to yourself, at a regular pace. Listen for natural pauses in your voice. These pauses separate words into meaningful units for speakers and listeners.

1. Sentence 3: **By following this advice I gained self-confidence.**

   Which correction should be made to sentence 3?

   (1) insert a comma after <u>following</u>
   (2) insert a comma after <u>advice</u>
   (3) insert a comma after <u>gained</u>
   (4) insert a comma after <u>By</u>
   (5) no correction is necessary

2. Sentence 5: **I say what I mean, and I get what I want.**

   Which correction should be made to sentence 5?

   (1) add a comma after <u>I say</u>
   (2) add a comma after <u>I get</u>
   (3) remove the comma after <u>I mean</u>
   (4) change the comma to a semicolon
   (5) no correction is necessary

UNIT 5

Directions: Choose the <u>one best answer</u> to each question.

<u>Questions 3 through 5</u> refer to the following information.

Choosing Fresh Produce

(A)

(1) You've joined others in the grocery store I'm sure who were thumping watermelons or smelling cantaloupes in an effort to choose the best produce. (2) Yet we've all experienced the disappointment of biting into a slice of watermelon or apple that wasn't sweet. (3) What is the secret to selecting produce that is ripe sweet crisp or juicy? (4) Here are a few tips that may help.

(B)

(5) First, use your eyes. (6) Don't buy any produce that contains bruises, wrinkles, mold, holes, rust, or slime. (7) Next, use your nose. (8) Don't buy any produce that doesn't smell good.

(C)

(9) Now that you know what not buy, let's turn our attention to the remaining produce. (10) Buy medium-sized, fleshy produce that is in season. (11) If possible buy local produce. (12) In general, the less time the produce spent en route to your supermarket, the better.

(D)

(13) Here's a buying guide for a few favorites:

PRODUCE	CHARACTERISTICS
asparagus	tight, green stalks, purple buds
broccoli	tight, green, firm
corn	tight, green, moist
grapes	fat, complete color, firm attachments
peaches	creamy yellow, no bruises, no wrinkles
strawberries	bright, fat, fragrant

---

3. Sentence 1: **You've joined others in the grocery store I'm sure who were thumping watermelons or smelling cantaloupes in an effort to choose the best produce.**

   Which correction should be made to sentence 1?

   (1) insert a comma after <u>joined</u>
   (2) insert a comma after <u>store</u> and after <u>who</u>
   (3) insert a comma after <u>watermelons</u>
   (4) insert a comma after <u>store</u> and after <u>sure</u>
   (5) no correction is necessary

4. Sentence 3: **What is the secret to selecting produce that is ripe sweet crisp or juicy?**

   Which correction should be made to sentence 3?

   (1) replace <u>What is</u> with <u>What's</u>
   (2) insert commas in a series after <u>ripe</u> <u>sweet</u> and <u>crisp</u>
   (3) replace <u>to</u> with <u>too</u>
   (4) insert a comma after <u>or</u>
   (5) no correction is necessary

5. Sentence 11: **If possible buy local produce.**

   Which correction should be made to sentence 11?

   (1) change <u>buy</u> to <u>by</u>
   (2) insert <u>you should</u> after <u>possible</u>
   (3) insert a comma after <u>possible</u>
   (4) insert a comma after <u>If</u>
   (5) no correction is necessary

Other Punctuation

Mechanics

A _____
" _____ .
_____
_____ "

① Learn the Skill

Punctuation includes commas (,), end marks (. ! ?), semicolons (;), colons (:), apostrophes ('), hyphens (-), dashes (–), parentheses ( ), and quotation marks (""), and helps readers understand a writer's intended meaning. Consider the following example without punctuation: *Did Bud the coach say I positioned myself on the playing field and began calling the players names yesterday;* and with punctuation: *Did Bud, the coach, say "I positioned myself on the playing field and began calling the player's names," yesterday?*

② Practice the Skill

By mastering the skill of using punctuation effectively, you will improve your writing and test-taking skills, especially as they relate to the GED Language Arts/Writing Test. Read the paragraph and strategies below. Then answer the question that follows.

A Use a hyphen when combining modifiers: *reddish-blonde* = the blonde hair has red in it; *man-eating shark* = the shark eats man.

B Use quotation marks around the exact words of a person or around the title of a small work contained within a larger work.

C Use a colon after an independent clause that introduces an example or a list: *This is an example, therefore we can use a colon.*

(A)

(1) When you say no, mean it, Mrs. Morgan, my former U.S. History teacher, laughed as she brushed a strand of **reddish-blond** hair from her eyes. (2) We were standing together in the hallway outside one wing of my old school. (3) The warm afternoon sun kept us from other obligations. (4) **"That's** one thing I always tried to do with my kids. (5) I didn't want to send the message that I didn't mean what I said. (6) If people think you don't mean what you say, they will take advantage of **you,"** she finished, giving me a motherly look. (7) Although I didn't know it at the time, this piece of advice would change my life in a positive **way:** it helped with my uncle, my dog, and my future.

✓ TEST-TAKING TIPS

Make sure that every sentence contains an end mark. Next, examine each sentence's internal structure to identify that other punctuation is used correctly.

1. Sentence 1: **When you say no, mean it, Mrs. Morgan, my former U.S. History teacher, laughed as she brushed a strand of reddish-blond hair from her eyes.**

   Which correction should be made to sentence 1?

   (1) insert a semicolon after <u>mean it</u>
   (2) remove the comma after <u>Morgan</u>
   (3) replace the period after <u>eyes</u> with an exclamation point
   (4) insert quotation marks around <u>When you say no, mean it,</u>
   (5) no correction is necessary

UNIT 5

Directions: Choose the <u>one best answer</u> to each question.

<u>Questions 2 through 4</u> refer to the following information.

CALL TO ACTION
Foster Healthy Diet Choices in Young People

(A)

(1) The American Association of Pediatrics, among other related organizations, calls on the nation's public and private schools to foster healthy diet choices in young people. (2) Healthy diet choices promote heart health and fight diseases such as diabetes. (3) Dr. Harvey Jones says Teaching our children to eat well is the most important thing we can do for them. (4) To this end, the AAP will provide information and support services to any school that makes healthy eating a priority.

REMEDY FOR RE-THINKING EATING
Take Ten

(B)

(5) To begin, take ten minutes to form a school- and community-based committee to address the following subject areas and focus questions as they relate to your school

- Eating environment—(6) Where and when do students eat? (7) Does the environment promote nutrition?
- Funding—(8) What local, state, or federal monies are available to promote nutrition.
- Integrated curriculum—(9) How can nutrition be reinforced in every subject area?
- Meeting nutrition standards—(10) Do the students meet daily nutrition standards?
- Accessibility of healthy food—(11) Are healthy foods easily accessible to students?
- Role models—(12) What message do adult eating habits send students with regard to nutrition?
- Healthy snacks—(13) Is nutrition promoted during snack or nutrition breaks?
- Making nutrition the focus of food sales—(14) Do all food sales by the school or school support groups promote nutrition over profit?

---

2. Sentence 3: **Dr. Harvey Jones says Teaching our children to eat well is the most important thing we can do for them.**

   Which correction should be made to sentence 3?

   (1) insert a colon after <u>says</u>
   (2) insert a comma after <u>says</u> and quotation marks around Dr. Jones's words
   (3) replace the period with an exclamation point
   (4) insert a comma after <u>children</u>
   (5) no correction is necessary

3. Sentence 5: **To begin, take ten minutes to form a school- and community-based committee to address the following subject areas and focus questions as they relate to your school**

   Which correction should be made to sentence 5?

   (1) insert a semicolon after <u>focus questions</u>
   (2) remove the hyphen from <u>community-based</u>
   (3) insert a colon after <u>your school</u>
   (4) remove the comma after <u>To begin</u>
   (5) no correction is necessary

4. Sentence 8: **What local, state, or federal monies are available to promote nutrition.**

   Which correction should be made to sentence 8?

   (1) replace the period with a question mark
   (2) change <u>monies</u> to <u>moneys</u>
   (3) remove the comma after <u>local</u>
   (4) insert a hyphen between <u>federal</u> and <u>monies</u>
   (5) no correction is necessary

Unit 5 Review

The Unit Review is structured to resemble the GED Language Arts/Writing Test. Be sure to read each question and all possible answers very carefully before choosing your answer.

To record your answers, fill in the numbered circle that corresponds to the answer you select for each question in the Unit Review.

Do not rest your pencil on the answer area while considering your answer. Make no stray or unnecessary marks. If you change an answer, erase your first mark completely.

Mark only one answer space for each question; multiple answers will be scored as incorrect.

Sample Question

Sentence 2: **The label can be easily read yet understanding the label can be challenging.**

Which correction should be made to sentence 2?

(1) remove <u>yet</u>
(2) insert a comma after <u>read</u>
(3) change <u>can be</u> to <u>can't be</u>
(4) replace the period with an exclamation point
(5) no correction is necessary

Directions: Choose the <u>one best answer</u> to each question.

<u>Questions 1 through 6</u> refer to the following information.

Sample Nutrition Label

Nutrition Facts

Serving Size 1 potato (148g/5.3oz)

Amount Per Serving	
Calories 100	Calories from Fat 0

	% Daily Value*
Total Fat 0g	**0%**
Saturated Fat 0g	**0%**
Cholesterol 0mg	**0%**
Sodium 0mg	**0%**
Potassium 720mg	**21%**
Total Carbohydrate 26g	**9%**
Dietary Fiber 3g	**12%**
Sugars 3g	
Protein 4g	

Vitamin A 0%	Vitamin C 45%
Calcium 2%	Iron 6%
Thiamin 8%	Riboflavin 2%
Niacin 8%	Vitamin B$_6$ 10%
Folate 6%	Phosphorous 6%
Zinc 2%	Magnesium 6%

*Percent Daily Values are based on a 2,000 calorie diet.

(A)

(1) The Nutrition Label on a food product is easy to find and read. (2) Yet, understanding the label can be challenging. (3) first note the serving size at the top of the label (4) All the information that follows relates to the serving size; 100 calories in one serving, 200 calories in two servings, 300 calories in three servings, and so on.

(B)

(5) Next, differentiate between the "good" ingredients and the "bad" ingredients. (6) The "bad" ingredients such as fat, cholesterol, and sodium are listed first. (7) You will want to limit your intake of these items. (8) The % daily value number will help you accomplish this goal. (9) Use this rule of thumb when interpreting % daily value numbers: 5% is low and 20% is high. (10) For example, 21% potassium is a bad high number.

(C)

(11) The "good' ingredients, such as vitamins, calcium, and iron, are listed last. (12) You want to increase you're intake of these items. (13) Again, the % daily value number will help you accomplish this goal. (14) For example, 45% vitamin C is a good high number.

1. Sentence 1: **The Nutrition Label on a food product is easy to find and read.**

   Which correction should be made to sentence 1?

   (1) replace <u>Nutrition Label</u> with <u>nutrition label</u>
   (2) insert a comma after <u>Label</u>
   (3) replace <u>read</u> with <u>reed</u>
   (4) insert <u>to</u> before <u>read</u>
   (5) no correction is necessary

   ① ② ③ ④ ⑤

2. Sentence 3: **first note the serving size at the top of the label**

   Which is the best way to write sentence 3? If the original is the best way, choose option (1).

   (1) first note the serving size at the top of the label
   (2) First note the serving size at the top of the label
   (3) first note the serving size at the top of the label.
   (4) first, note the serving size at the top of the label.
   (5) First, note the serving size at the top of the label.

   ① ② ③ ④ ⑤

3. Sentence 4: **All the information that follows relates to the serving size; 100 calories in one serving, 200 calories in two servings, 300 calories in three servings, and so on.**

   Which correction should be made to sentence 4?

   (1) remove the semicolon
   (2) change the semicolon to a colon
   (3) replace <u>All</u> with <u>all</u>
   (4) remove the series of commas
   (5) no correction is necessary

   ① ② ③ ④ ⑤

4. Sentence 7: <u>**You will**</u> **want to limit your intake of these items.**

   Which is the correct contraction of the underlined portion of the sentence?

   (1) You're
   (2) Your'e
   (3) You'll
   (4) Youl'l
   (5) You'ill

   ① ② ③ ④ ⑤

5. Sentence 11: **The "good' ingredients, such as vitamins, calcium, and iron, are listed last.**

   Which correction should be made to sentence 11?

   (1) change the period to a question mark
   (2) change <u>"good'</u> to <u>"good"</u>
   (3) insert a comma after <u>such as</u>
   (4) change <u>"good'</u> to <u>good'</u>
   (5) no correction is necessary

   ① ② ③ ④ ⑤

6. Sentence 12: **You want to increase you're intake of these items.**

   Which correction should be made to sentence 12?

   (1) remove <u>You want to</u>
   (2) replace <u>items</u> with <u>item's</u>
   (3) insert a colon after <u>intake</u>
   (4) replace <u>you're</u> with <u>your</u>
   (5) no correction is necessary

   ① ② ③ ④ ⑤

Directions: Choose the <u>one best answer</u> to each question.

<u>Questions 7 through 12</u> refer to the following information.

Cancer Prevention

(A)

(1) Oral cancer affects about 1 out of every 98 people. (2) To prevent this common cancer, report persistent mouth sores to your doctor. (3) In addition, report signs of color change, pain, tenderness, or numbness in the mouth. (4) Limit or eliminate smoking and drinking alcohol. (5) Use sunscreen on your lips. (6) Finally, it is valueble to eat avocados. (7) Research suggests that chemicals in avocados destroy oral cancer cells.

(B)

(8) Leukemia affects children and older adults. (9) Report the following symptoms to your doctor immediately: paleness, bruising, bleeding gums, tiredness, odd fevers, or bone or joint discomfort. (10) As a preventative measure limit the number of CT scans you undergo. (11) Excess radiation may trigger leukemia.

(C)

(12) Endometrial or uterine cancer affects about 1 out of every 40 women. (13) Most cases affect women older then 50. (14) Report the following symptoms to your doctor immediately uncommon bleeding or pelvic pain. (15) Its also important to report one's family medical history to a physician. (16) To prevent endometrial cancer, maintain a healthy weight, exercise, and replace iron supplements with calcium supplements after age 50.

---

7. Sentence 2: **To prevent this common cancer, report persistent mouth sores to your doctor.**

   Which correction should be made to sentence 2?

   (1) replace To with Too
   (2) remove the comma after cancer
   (3) change sores to soars
   (4) change doctor to Doctor
   (5) no correction is necessary

   ①②③④⑤

8. Sentence 6: **Finally, it is valueble to eat avocados.**

   Which correction should be made to sentence 6?

   (1) change valueble to valuable
   (2) change valueble to valued
   (3) replace Finally with Finaly
   (4) replace it is with its
   (5) no correction is necessary

   ①②③④⑤

9. Sentence 10: **As a preventative measure limit the number of CT scans you undergo.**

   Which correction should be made to sentence 10?

   (1) insert a comma after measure
   (2) replace scans with scan's
   (3) insert a colon after undergo
   (4) replace CT with ct
   (5) no correction is necessary

   ①②③④⑤

10. Sentence 13: **Most cases affect women older then 50.**

    Which correction should be made to sentence 13?

    (1) change affect to effect
    (2) change women to woman
    (3) replace then with than
    (4) replace cases with case's
    (5) no correction is necessary

    ①②③④⑤

11. Sentence 14: **Report the following symptoms to your doctor immediately uncommon bleeding or pelvic pain.**

    Which correction should be made to sentence 14?

    (1) remove following
    (2) insert a colon after immediately
    (3) replace your with you're
    (4) change uncommon to uncomon
    (5) no correction is necessary

    ①②③④⑤

12. Sentence 15: **Its also important to report one's family medical history to a physician.**

    Which correction should be made to sentence 15?

    (1) change Its to It's
    (2) replace important with inportant
    (3) replace important with importent
    (4) replace one's with ones
    (5) no correction is necessary

    ①②③④⑤

Questions 13 through 18 refer to the following letter.

Money Bank
200 North Street
Chapel Hill, NC 55555
(919) 555–6237

Mr. Paul Wilford
1234 Kettle Street
Chapel Hill, NC 55555

Dear Mr. Wilford:

(A)
    (1) First, let me express my appreciation that you have chosen our bank to serve your financial needs upon your relocation to texarkana. (2) We strive to provide our customers with quality services that satisfy every aspect of their financial portfolios, including savings, bill payment, and education and retirement funds.

(B)
    (3) In response to your inquiry regarding a checking account, the following items are necessary to open such an account. (4) Two forms of identification, including one with a picture: your social security number: and a $300 deposit. (5) Once you've gathered these items, one of our financial advisor's will be happy to assist you in opening a checking account. (6) Please consider the option of opening a companion savings account as well. (7) The too accounts will guarantee that you have many options as you manage your monthly expenses.

(C)
    (8) Please don't hesitate to contact me if you have other questions. (9) We look forward to serving you.

Sincerely,

Ima Bennet, Manager

13. Sentence 1: **First, let me express my appreciation that you have chosen our bank to serve your financial needs upon your relocation to texarkana.**

Which of the following words from sentence 1 should be capitalized?

(1) bank
(2) texarkana
(3) financial
(4) relocation
(5) express

①②③④⑤

14. Sentence 3: **In response to your inquiry regarding a checking account, the following items are necessary to open such an account.**

Which correction should be made to sentence 3?

(1) change your to you're
(2) replace the period with a colon
(3) change are to our
(4) change inquiry to inquary
(5) no correction is necessary

①②③④⑤

15. Sentence 4: **Two forms of identification, including one with a picture: your social security number: and a $300 deposit.**

Which correction should be made to sentence 4?

(1) change the colons to semicolons
(2) replace Two with Too
(3) remove the comma after identification
(4) change forms to form's
(5) no correction is necessary

①②③④⑤

16. Sentence 5: **Once you've gathered these items, one of our financial advisor's will be happy to assist you in opening a checking account.**

Which correction should be made to sentence 5?

(1) replace you've with you're
(2) change the comma to a colon
(3) replace advisor's with advisors
(4) change gathered to gather
(5) no correction is necessary

①②③④⑤

17. Sentence 7: **The too accounts will guarantee that you have many options as you manage your monthly expenses.**

Which correction should be made to sentence 7?

(1) remove monthly
(2) insert a semicolon after options
(3) change guarantee to gaurantee
(4) replace too with two
(5) no correction is necessary

①②③④⑤

18. Sentence 9: **We look forward to serving you.**

Which correction should be made to sentence 9?

(1) change We to They
(2) replace forward with fourward
(3) replace to with too
(4) change serving to serve
(5) no correction is necessary

①②③④⑤

Answer Key

UNIT 1 ESSAY

LESSON 1, *pp. 2–3*

1. (4), This sentence states the topic of the essay.

Prompt 1, The thesis statement should include a specific invention that is important to you: *The invention that is most important to me is the car.*

Prompt 2, The thesis statement should include the month or time of year (season) that you like best: *Fall is my favorite season.*

Prompt 3, The thesis statement should include a plant, animal, or weather condition found in nature that you like best: *My favorite animal is the giraffe.*

Prompt 4, The thesis statement should include your favorite learning method or technique: *I am an auditory learner and like to hear things as I am being taught.*

LESSON 2, *pp. 4–5*

1. (5), This sentence introduces the three details that support the thesis.

Prompt 1, The introductory paragraph should include a hook, thesis statement, and three supporting details about an invention that is important to you.

Prompt 2, The introductory paragraph should include a hook, thesis statement, and three supporting details about your favorite month or time of year (season).

LESSON 3, *pp. 6–7*

1. (2), This sentence uses the transitioning phrase, "It was around this time," which shows time.

Prompt, The thesis statement should include a specific invention that is important to you: *The invention that is most important to me is the car.* The two supporting details should be examples or reasons why the invention is important to you: *Having a car means I can get to where I need to go, and it also gives me a sense of freedom.* Each body paragraph should be about one of the supporting details and begin with a transition. Possible transitions include *When, Later, First,* and *Another.*

LESSON 4, *pp. 8–9*

1. (1), This sentence goes into more detail about the little beagle that the writer saw in the window. This is elaboration.

Prompt, The thesis statement should be the same as on page 3, unless you want to rewrite it: *The invention that is most important to me is the car.* The third supporting detail should be the third detail that supports your thesis statement: *My family works in the auto industry.* The body paragraph should

include elaboration of the supporting detail. Explain why this detail supports the thesis statement and give examples: *Another example of how the invention of the car is important to me is because the auto manufacturing plant in my city has provided my dad and several other family members with high-paying jobs for years.*

LESSON 5, *pp. 10–11*

1. (2), The conclusion ends with an insightful thought because it provides the reader with insight into the writer's life. The last sentence is not a quote, is not advice, is not an apology, and does not discuss how much the writer likes working with dogs.

2. (5), This sentence restates the thesis statement without copying it word for word. The other options do not restate the thesis statement because they show elaboration, transition, and supporting details.

Prompt 1, The concluding paragraph should end the essay about the invention that is most important to you. It should include a transition, restate the thesis and supporting details, and leave a lasting impression.

Prompt 2, The concluding paragraph is about a responsibility and why it is important in your life. It should include a transition, restate the thesis and supporting details, and leave a lasting impression.

LESSON 6, *pp. 12–15*

Practice, The essay is missing a paragraph transition and transitions between sentences. It is also missing elaboration. For example, *A few months after joining the tennis class, I noticed that I felt healthier. I realized then that tennis is a great way to stay in shape. We spend a lot of time exercising when we play. Also, during practice we run laps around the court to warm up. Then we do sprints. During our practice games, we have to run laps if we hit a ball out of bounds. That's okay though, because it keeps me fit, and it feels good.*

Write, Paragraph B needs to be indented and is missing a transition. It could read: *My dog is inside most of the day, so she lacks exercise.* The writer uses the words "I think." It should read: *She really enjoys it, and it keeps her healthy.* Paragraph C should elaborate on why the trails, trees, and lake are important to the writer. Paragraph D combines the third body paragraph and the conclusion. They should be separate, indented paragraphs. The conclusion is missing a supporting detail: *I spend quality time outside, I meet a lot of new people, and my dog gets the exercise she needs.* The conclusion also uses the words "I think." Instead, write a sentence that expresses something gained: *Ever since we started coming to the dog park, my dog and I have developed a strong bond.*

Review, Double-check your essay to ensure that it meets the criteria for the GED Language Arts/Writing Test.

Revise, Rewrite any portions of your essay that do not meet the criteria of the GED Language Arts/Writing Test.

UNIT 1 (continued)

UNIT 1 REVIEW, *pp. 16–19*

Prompt 1, The larger bubble is the thesis statement: *I was most scared the time that my car slid on the ice while I was driving in the snow.* The three smaller bubbles are your three supporting details: *It was Christmas Eve and I was on the way to meet my family; Two trucks stopped, and the drivers pushed my car back to the road; The only damage that was caused was a flat tire.*

Prompt 2, Draw a mental map in the space provided. The larger bubble is the thesis statement: *Generosity is a characteristic that makes a good neighbor.* The three smaller bubbles are your three supporting details: *My neighbor brought me soup when I was sick; She gave me my favorite candy on Christmas; All of my neighbors teamed up to throw a giant block party.*

Prompt 3, Draw a mental map in the space provided. The larger bubble is the thesis statement: *My most indispensible possession is my computer.* The three smaller bubbles are your three supporting details: *I need my computer to access emails; Without my computer I would not be able to share photos and stories with friends and family who live far away; Having a computer allows me to work from home.*

Prompt 4, Draw a mental map in the space provided. The larger bubble is the thesis statement: *My father has always had good manners, especially at dinner.* The three smaller bubbles are your three supporting details: *My father never puts his elbows on the table; My father always takes his hat off when he is inside; My father makes sure to say please and thank you.*

UNIT 2 ORGANIZATION

LESSON 1, *pp. 22–23*

1. (4), Sentence 6 should begin paragraph E because it is the conclusion. The conclusion indicates a change in scene from a telephone conversation to a reflection of events.

2. (4), Sentence 4 should begin paragraph B because paragraph B shifts its focus to the first supporting detail. Sentence 4 refers to the first supporting detail.

3. (5), Sentence 7 should begin paragraph C because paragraph C shifts its focus to the second supporting detail. Sentence 7 refers to the second supporting detail.

4. (1), Sentence 11 expresses a shift from supporting details to summary or reflection. Therefore, it should begin a concluding paragraph.

LESSON 2, *pp. 24–25*

1. (2), This sentence states the topic, identifies the writer's perspective, and provides a transition between paragraphs D and E. The other answer options do not provide the transition or information necessary for an effective topic sentence.

2. (3), This sentence is the topic sentence because it introduces the topic of voting qualifications.

3. (4), This sentence is the topic sentence because it introduces the topic of obtaining and filing voter registration forms, which is what the paragraph is about.

4. (5), This sentence is the topic sentence because it introduces the topic of completely filling out the voter registration forms, which is what the paragraph is about.

LESSON 3, *pp. 26–27*

1. (1), This sentence is the supporting detail because it supports the topic of the writer meaning what he or she says and why.

2. (4), This sentence is the supporting detail because it supports the topic of identifying the vacationing interests of the family.

3. (1), This sentence is the supporting detail because it supports the topic of determining a budget for the family vacation.

4. (3), This sentence is the supporting detail because it supports the topic of how much time the vacationers will want to spend traveling.

LESSON 4, *pp. 28–29*

1. (3), The phrase "Although I didn't know it at the time" is a transition because it shows time. It indicates that the advice took place in the past.

2. (2), "For example" provides a transition from sentence 5 to sentence 6.

3. (4), "However" indicates a contrast to the previous statement, therefore providing a transition between sentences.

4. (1), "In contrast" indicates a contrast to the previous statement, therefore providing a transition between sentences.

LESSON 5, *pp. 30–31*

1. (1), Sentence 4 should be removed because it does not relate to the topic.

2. (4), Sentence 4 should follow sentence 7 because that is the point in the paragraph where new fixtures are discussed. As it is now, the sentence introduces an idea in the wrong place.

3. (2), Sentence 16 should be removed because it does not relate to the topic.

4. (3), Sentence 22 should be removed because it does not relate to the topic.

UNIT REVIEW, *pp. 32–37*

1. (4), "However" indicates a contrast to the previous statement, thus providing a transition between sentences. The other answer options indicate similarities.

2. (1), Sentence 4 should be moved to the beginning of paragraph B because the idea has shifted, and sentence 4 better relates to the topic of paragraph B.

3. (4), "Next, you'll need a liquid" is a transitional phrase that moves the reader to the next paragraph and introduces a new detail. The other answer options do not contain transitions.

UNIT 2 (*continued*)

4. (2), "Finally" indicates that this is the last step of making a smoothie and has transitioned the reader to the last paragraph. The other answer options do not indicate time.

5. (1), This sentence provides more information regarding the topic of protein powder, vitamins, and herbs as a healthy supplement. Answer option 3 may seem like the right answer because it also references the topic; however this sentence provides unnecessary information and does not stay on the overall topic of smoothie nutrition.

6. (3), "Then" is a transitional word that shows time. The other answer options do not show time.

7. (3), Sentence 3 should be removed because it does not relate to the topic.

8. (1), Sentence 5 should begin paragraph B because it introduces the next idea and provides a transition between paragraphs.

9. (2), "Next, gather supplies and tools for the job" is a transitional phrase that introduces a new idea.

10. (1), "Finally" is a transitional word that indicates time and begins the final paragraph; therefore no correction is necessary.

11. (5), This sentence does not interrupt the unity and coherence of the paragraph. It connects sentences 12 and 14. The other answer options do not fit within the paragraph.

12. (4), Sentence 16 should follow sentence 14 because that is the point in the paragraph where preparing the walls is discussed. As it is now, the sentence introduces an idea in the wrong place.

13. (2), "Understandably" indicates empathy from the writer to the reader about the perceived daunting task of buying a new camera, thus transitioning from one sentence to the next. The other answer options indicate time, contrast, and explanation.

14. (2), "Hopefully" indicates empathy from the writer to the reader about the steps that can be taken to make buying a camera a little less daunting. The other answer options indicate time and contrast; therefore they cannot be correct.

15. (3), Sentence 7 should be removed because it does not relate to the topic.

16. (4), Sentence 9 should begin paragraph C because it introduces the next idea and provides a transition between paragraphs.

17. (5), This sentence is the topic sentence of paragraph D. The other answer options do not relate to the topic of the paragraph; therefore they cannot be correct.

18. (1), "However" indicates contrast to the previous statement, thus providing a transition between sentences. The other answer options indicate time and explanation; therefore no correction is necessary.

UNIT 3 SENTENCE STRUCTURE

LESSON 1, *pp. 40–41*

1. (2), "But" is the correct transition; however, it should connect to sentence 4 with a comma. Therefore, option 2 is correct, and the other answer options are not.

2. (1), "Such as" should not begin a sentence. This sentence cannot stand alone; therefore it must be connected to the previous sentence.

3. (3), Sentence 9 is missing end punctuation and is asking a question, so the end punctuation should be a question mark.

4. (4), Sentence 14 is not asking a question; therefore the question mark should be changed to a period.

5. (5), Sentence 18 contains all the necessary parts of a complete sentence, including the correct end punctuation; therefore no correction is necessary.

LESSON 2, *pp. 42–43*

1. (2), Sentence 7 begins with the conjunction "Although," which indicates that it is a sentence fragment and must be connected to another sentence in order to be complete.

2. (2), Sentence 2 begins with "But," which indicates that it is a sentence fragment and must be connected to another sentence in order to be complete.

3. (4), Sentence 6 begins with "However," which indicates that it is a fragment and must be connected to another sentence in order to be complete.

4. (5), Sentence 13 begins with "If" and, in this case, cannot stand alone. Therefore, it must be connected to another sentence in order to form a complete idea.

LESSON 3, *pp. 44–45*

1. (1), "I" is a subject and "changed" is a verb. The subject performs the action, and the action is the verb.

2. (4), Sentence 4 contains one subject, one verb, and a single idea; therefore it is a simple sentence.

3. (1), "Includes" is the action in the sentence; therefore it is a verb.

4. (2), Sentence 14 is a sentence fragment that contains the same information as sentence 15. Therefore, it is not necessary and should be removed.

LESSON 4, *pp. 46–47*

1. (3), The coordinating conjunction "but" combines the two independent clauses; therefore sentence 3 and 4 form a compound sentence.

2. (2), The two independent clauses are connected by a semicolon (forming a compound sentence).

3. (4), "And" is a coordinating conjunction.

4. (1), This is a compound sentence because it contains a semicolon between two independent clauses, as well as the conjunctive adverb "however."

UNIT 3 (continued)

LESSON 5, *pp. 48–49*

1. (2), Sentence 1 is a dependent clause and needs to be attached to an independent clause, such as sentence 2. Because the sentences are not both independent clauses, they cannot be combined with a semicolon; therefore they must be combined with a comma.

2. (4), The sentence contains both an independent clause and a dependent clause; therefore the sentence is complex.

3. (2), "While" is a subordinating conjunction because it introduces the dependent clause.

4. (3), Sentence 20 is a dependent clause and needs to be attached to an independent clause, such as sentence 21. Because the sentences are not both independent clauses, they cannot be combined with a semicolon; therefore they must be combined with a comma.

LESSON 6, *pp. 50–51*

1. (3), The sentences are combined by eliminating repetitive words, such as "wanted," without changing the meaning of the sentence. Using the conjunction "and" creates a compound sentence.

2. (3), The sentences are combined using the conjunction "and" which creates a compound sentence.

3. (1), The sentences are combined by eliminating repetitive words, such as "An emergency may include," from sentences 4 and 5. Using the conjunction "and" creates one complete sentence.

LESSON 7, *pp. 52–53*

1. (2), The coordinating conjunction "but" corrects this comma-splice by forming a compound sentence.

2. (3), The semicolon corrects the comma-splice by forming a compound sentence.

3. (5), Adding the subordinating conjunction "When" and the comma after "provider" corrects the run-on sentence by forming a complex sentence.

4. (1), The comma and coordinating conjunction "and" correct this run-on sentence by forming a compound sentence

LESSON 8, *pp. 54–55*

1. (1), The word that should be modified is "choosing"; therefore the modifier "carefully" should precede it.

2. (3), The modifying phrase "in the background" is intended for the music, not the cactuses.

3. (1), The word that should be modified is "tacos"; therefore the modifier "spicy" should precede it.

4. (4), The modifying word "systematically" refers to the building of the tacos, not to the flavor combinations; therefore "systematically" should follow "tacos."

LESSON 9, *pp. 56–57*

1. (2), In sentence 1, the modifier "value" is incorrectly used as a subject, creating a dangling modifier (no subject to modify). The intended subject is "advice." Answer option 2 is the best revision of sentence 1 because the subject is correctly modified within a complete sentence.

2. (3), In sentence 2, the modifier "obtained" is incorrectly modifying the word "physicals." The intended subject is "employees." Answer option 3 is the best revision of sentence 2 because the subject is correctly modified.

3. (1), Sentence 4 is missing the subject of the employer-sponsored wellness programs. The intended subject is "employees." Answer option 1 is the best revision of sentence 4 because the subject is correctly modified.

4. (4), The missing subject is "employees" because "the paper-work and physicals must be completed" by the employees.

LESSON 10, *pp. 58–59*

1. (3), "Achieved" and "stood" maintain parallel structure because they both indicate past tense.

2. (3), "To give instruction" and "to enlighten" maintain parallel structure because they are both *to+verb* forms.

3. (1), "Bargaining" and "negotiating" maintain parallel structure because they both end in the suffix –*ing*.

4. (4), "Personalize" and "humanize" maintain parallel structure because they are both in present tense and in the same verb form.

UNIT REVIEW, *pp. 60–65*

1. (1), Sentences 1, 2, and 3 are simple sentences that are better stated if combined. Answer option 1 combines the sentences by eliminating repetitive words, such as "will" and "the," without changing its meaning.

2. (3), Sentences 5, 6, and 7 are combined by eliminating repetitive words such as "replacement sets" to form a complex sentence without changing its meaning.

3. (2), Sentence 8 is a dependent clause because it does not state a complete idea; therefore it must be combined with sentence 9 to form a complex sentence. Because the sentences are not both independent clauses, a coordinating conjunction is not necessary.

4. (5), Sentence 11 is a dependent clause because it does not state a complete idea; therefore it must be combined with sentence 12 to form a complex sentence. A semicolon and colon are not necessary because the sentences are not both independent clauses, nor do they show an example or list.

5. (2), The colon at the end of sentence 13 indicates that a list should follow.

6. (2), Sentence 1 is a dependent clause because it does not state a complete idea; therefore it must be combined with sentence 2 to form a complex sentence. A semicolon and coordinating conjunction are not necessary because the sentences are not both independent clauses.

UNIT 3 (continued)

7. (1), Sentence 3 is an independent clause, but sentence 4 is dependent. They must be combined to form one complete sentence. Answer option 1 is the only option to combine the two sentences into one complete sentence without dangling or misplaced modifiers.

8. (2), Two clauses are combined without a conjunction or punctuation; therefore it is a run-on sentence.

9. (3), Sentences 9 and 10 are combined by eliminating repetitive words such as "Copies of the company letter of transmittal" from sentence 10 to form a compound sentence without changing its meaning.

10. (4), This sentence contains one subject, one verb, and one idea; therefore it is a simple sentence.

11. (2), The word "narrowing" and "hardening" maintain parallel structure because they both end in the suffix *–ing*.

12. (2), The word "does" is present tense and "allowing" is a present participle. The tenses do not match; therefore "allowing" should change to the present tense *allow*.

13. (3), Sentence 6 is missing a subject. Answer option 3 is the only option that includes the person doing the action (eating or keeping his or her heart healthy).

14. (4), The word "only" is modifying the eating of good fats. The writer is not intending to suggest that the reader eat good fats and nothing else, but that the reader eat good fats rather than bad fats; therefore "only" should follow "eat."

15. (5), The sentence does not contain any errors; therefore no correction is necessary.

UNIT 4 USAGE

LESSON 1, pp. 68–69

1. (4), "Mrs." is a title and "Morgan" and "U.S." are proper names. Titles and proper names should always be capitalized.

2. (2), "Italy," "Spain," and "France" are proper names that must be capitalized.

3. (3), "Eiffel Tower" is the specific name of a specific thing; therefore it is a proper noun and must be capitalized.

4. (1), The noun "books" is not a proper name and does not begin the sentence; therefore it should not be capitalized.

5. (1), This sentence does not contain any errors; therefore the original is the best answer option.

LESSON 2, pp. 70–71

1. (4), "Uncle Joe" is the object of the verb "told." Replacing "Uncle Joe" with the object pronoun "him" is the best option.

2. (2), The noun "grandmother" appears in sentence 2 three times. The first time is okay, but the remaining nouns need to be replaced with pronouns. The second "grandmother" shows possession; therefore it should be replaced with the possessive pronoun "her." The third "grandmother" is used as the subject

of the verb "showed." It should be replaced with the subject pronoun "she."

3. (2), It is unnecessary to repeat the plural subject "Grandmother's parents." It should be replaced with the plural subject pronoun "they."

4. (1), The pronoun "you" indicates that the writer is speaking directly to the reader. In this context "you" is correct. The pronoun "it" is a subject pronoun that is replacing the statement made in the previous sentence. In this context, "it" is also correct. This sentence does not contain any errors; therefore the original is the best answer option.

5. (4), It is unnecessary to repeat the plural object "fans"; therefore it should be replaced with the plural object pronoun "them." Answer option 2 is not correct because if you replace "the referee" with "he," the reader will not understand to whom "he" refers.

LESSON 3, pp. 72–73

1. (3), "Uncle Joe and Aunt Mary" is the antecedent, which appears in sentence 5. The pronoun that best agrees is "they." Because both of them said they understood in sentence 5, it is clear that the narrator is referring to both Uncle Joe and Aunt Mary in sentence 6.

2. (4), The "dress code" is the antecedent; therefore the pronoun that best agrees is "it."

3. (2), The antecedent in this sentence is "school officials." Therefore, the pronoun that best agrees is "they."

4. (3), The antecedent in this sentence is "composers"; therefore the pronoun that best agrees is "their."

5. (4), Sentence 4 is missing the subject, which should be "composers." However, it is unnecessary to repeat the word composers; instead the sentence should be rephrased to include the plural subject pronoun "they."

LESSON 4, pp. 74–75

1. (2), The collective noun "group" takes the singular verb "has" because the group acts as one.

2. (5), The collective noun "team" takes the singular verb "stops" because the team acts as one.

3. (4), The collective noun "team" takes the singular verb "loses" because the team acts as one.

4. (3), The collective noun "group" takes the singular verb "comes" because the group acts as one.

5. (5), The collective noun "group" takes the plural verb "want" because the group members act independently.

LESSON 5, pp. 76–77

1. (2), Sentence 4 indicates past tense; therefore the verb "know" should be replaced with its past tense form "knew."

2. (1), Sentence 1 indicates present tense; therefore "were" should be replaced with its present tense form "are."

3. (3), Sentence 4 indicates future tense; therefore the helping verb "will" should precede the verb "provide."

UNIT 4 (continued)

4. (1), Sentence 3 indicates present tense; therefore "was" should be replaced with its present tense form "is."

5. (4), Sentence 5 indicates future tense; therefore the helping verb "will" should precede the verb "see."

LESSON 6, *pp. 78–79*

1. (1), Sentence 10 indicates past tense; therefore the suffix –*ed* should be added to the regular verb "retrieve" to change it to its past tense form "retrieved."

2. (5), Sentence 2 indicates past tense; therefore the present tense form "showing" should be changed to its past tense form "showed."

3. (3), The second part of sentence 3 indicates present tense; therefore the suffix –*ing* should be added to the regular verb "stand" to change it to its present tense form "standing."

4. (4), Sentence 4 indicates past tense; therefore the suffix –*ed* should be added to the regular verb "base" to change it to its past tense form "based."

5. (1), Sentence 6 indicates future tense and contains a helping verb. The sentence does not contain any errors; therefore the original is the best answer option.

LESSON 7, *pp. 80–81*

1. (2), The first part of sentence 5 is past-perfect because the writer gave Uncle Joe an answer before changing his or her mind; therefore "had" should precede the main verb "let."

2. (2), Sentence 2 is present perfect tense because the cats started running around in the past and continue to do so in the present; therefore "have" should precede the main verb "run."

3. (3), Sentence 5 indicates that the actions of the group in sentence 5 and in sentence 6 took place before another action (before dinner). Therefore, you should use the past perfect tense: *had napped.*

4. (3), Sentence 3 is past perfect tense because the dealer paid a price in the past, before changing the price for resale. Therefore, "have" should be replaced with "had."

5. (5), Sentence 5 is past perfect tense because dealers received rebates prior to the year coming to an end; therefore "has" should be replaced by "had" and "receive" should be replaced by "received."

LESSON 8, *pp. 82–83*

1. (1), Sentence 5 is past tense; therefore the irregular verb "say" should be replaced with its past tense form "said."

2. (4), Sentence 1 is past tense. The helping verb "have" indicates that the past participle should be used; therefore "write" should be replaced with its past participle "written."

3. (5), Sentence 2 is present perfect tense because the writer wore clothes in the past and continues to wear clothes in the present. Present-perfect tense suggests the use of the helping verb "have," which indicates that the sentence should use the past participle "worn" instead of the past tense form "wore."

4. (2), Sentence 2 is present perfect tense because the writer implies that the reader has tried to lose weight in the past, but gave up and has not tried again. Present-perfect tense suggests the use of the helping verb "have," which indicates that the sentence should use the past participle "given" instead of the past tense form "gave."

5. (3), Even though "brought" is the past tense form or past participle form of "bring," sentence 5 indicates present tense due to the use of the helping verb "have." "Have" indicates that the action is taking place in the present. For example, *I brought cookies* indicates past tense, while *I have brought cookies* indicates present tense.

LESSON 9, *pp. 84–85*

1. (4), "Mrs. Morgan" is a singular subject; therefore the singular verb "is" should be used.

2. (3), The paragraph references a new phone; therefore the plural subject "phones" should be changed to the singular subject "phone," which agrees with the singular verb "is."

3. (2), "Scientists and phone technicians" is a compound subject; therefore the verb that best agrees is the plural verb "test."

4. (3), The noun "policies" is a plural subject; therefore the verb that best agrees is the plural verb "are."

5. (1), The proper noun "Office Supply" is a singular subject; therefore the verb that best agrees is the singular verb "monitors."

LESSON 10, *pp. 86–87*

1. (4), "I" is a singular subject that is an exception to the subject-verb agreement rule because "I" takes the singular form of the verb "to be," as in *I am*; however, in most other cases "I" takes the plural verb form, such as *I go* or *I know*. In this case, the verb that best agrees is the plural verb "control."

2. (3), "Step 2" is a singular subject; therefore the verb that best agrees is the singular verb "is."

3. (4), "Dealer" should be replaced with the plural subject "Dealers" because the paragraph is talking about dealers in general, not a specific dealer. The verb that best agrees with the plural subject "dealers" is the past perfect tense verb form "had received" because the dealers received rebates prior to the year coming to an end.

4. (5), "Apple" should be replaced with "apples" because the paragraph is about more than one apple. The verb that best agrees with the plural subject "apples" is the plural verb "do."

5. (1), "Tastes" is a verb and "taste" is a subject. For example, *the apple tastes sweet* and *the apple has a sweet taste.*

UNIT 4 (continued)

UNIT REVIEW, pp. 88–93

1. (3), The pronoun "them" is the plural pronoun that represents more than one cat. "Are" is the plural, present-tense form of the verb *to be*.

2. (2), The word "animals" is a noun because it is a thing. Nouns represent people, places, and things.

3. (4), The pronoun "them" is the plural pronoun that represents more than one cat. It replaces cats in the sentence.

4. (5), This sentence does not contain any errors; therefore no correction is necessary.

5. (4), The letter is about cats. The verb form "are" is the plural, present tense form of the verb *to be*. The word "many" agrees with the verb "are," and "cats" is plural because there is more than one cat.

6. (5), The nouns "owners" and "animals" should be plural because the letter is speaking about more than one owner and more than one cat.

7. (2), The verb "used" changes to "use" because the information is written in present tense. The verb form "are" changes to "is" because the airtime is singular and "is" is the singular, present tense form of the verb *to be*.

8. (1), This sentence is missing the noun *bill*.

9. (4), The word "be" is a verb in its original form, which should always be preceded by the word *to*: *to be*. Instead, the verb should be modified to fit within the context of the sentence: "are."

10. (4), The verb "have" agrees with the subject "you."

11. (3), This sentence is missing the noun *units*.

12. (4), More than one unit forms a group; therefore "unit" should be changed to "units."

13. (1), This sentence does not contain any errors; therefore the original is the best answer option.

14. (1), In this case, a pronoun should not replace the noun because it is unknown if "the foreperson" is a he or she. "They" represents more than one person, which is incorrect in this sentence.

15. (5), This sentence does not contain any errors; therefore no correction is necessary.

16. (2), The verb "are" is the plural, present tense form of the verb *to be*. It should replace "is" in this sentence because "is" is singular and "discussions" is plural.

17. (1), There is only one jury; therefore "juries" should be changed to "jury."

18. (3), The noun "jury" is singular; therefore the plural verb form "have" should be changed to its singular form "has."

UNIT 5 MECHANICS

LESSON 1, pp. 96–97

1. (2), Uncle is a title, Joe and Little Rock are proper nouns; therefore they should always be capitalized.

2. (1), Months of the year are always capitalized; therefore "january" should be replaced with "January."

3. (3), United States Postal Service is a proper noun and must be capitalized.

4. (4), Answer option 4 is the best answer because both "pine trees" and "you'll" are not capitalized. Neither begins a sentence, are titles, holidays, or proper nouns.

LESSON 2, pp. 98–99

1. (2), The contraction "you're" is short for *you are*, and you wouldn't say *Don't change you are mind*. The correct word for sentence 7 is the possessive pronoun "your" to indicate possession of the intended subject's "mind."

2. (1), The word "windows" is a plural noun meaning more than one window. In the context of sentence 1, the window is not showing possession; therefore the apostrophe should be removed. Also, the last part of sentence 1 is a dependent clause; therefore a comma should be placed before the beginning of the dependent clause "such as a basement, bathroom, or hallway."

3. (4), The contraction "you're" is short for *you are*, and you wouldn't say *Use you are senses*. The correct word for sentence 5 is the possessive pronoun "your" to indicate possession of the intended subject's "senses."

4. (2), The noun "familys" is incorrect because in order to make the singular noun *family* a plural noun, you would need to change the suffix y to *–ies*. However, in the context of sentence 8, the noun is not intended to be plural, but rather to show possession of the disaster kit by one family; therefore an apostrophe should be added before the *s* to show the possession.

LESSON 3, pp. 100–101

1. (1), The words "no" and "know" from sentence 6 are homophones because they sound the same but have different meanings.

2. (4), The word "brake" should be replaced with "break" because a *brake* is a part of a car and to *break* means to get rid of or separate.

3. (3), The word "Won" should be replaced with "One" because *won* means to win at something and *one* refers to a number.

4. (3), The word "boarder" should be replaced with "border" because *boarder* means a person who boards and *border* refers to a boundary or outer edge.

UNIT 5 (continued)

LESSON 4, pp. 102–103

1. (3), The misspelled word in sentence 3 is "apreciated," which is spelled *appreciated*.

2. (2), The underlined portion of sentence 7 contains two misspelled words: *laboratories* and *beneficial*. Answer option 2 is the best answer because not only are the words spelled correctly, but also the correct verb "suggests" is used: *The research suggests*, rather than *The research suggest*.

3. (5), Sentence 10 does not contain misspelled words, therefore no correction is necessary.

4. (2), The misspelled word in sentence 15 is "contraversy," which should be spelled *controversy*.

LESSON 5, pp. 104–105

1. (2), A comma should be inserted after "advice," because "By following this advice" is an introductory phrase. Introductory phrases can also be dependent clauses.

2. (5), Sentence 5 is a compound sentence and does not contain any comma errors; therefore no correction is necessary.

3. (4), Commas should be inserted after the words "store" and "sure" because "I'm sure" is an interrupting phrase.

4. (2), Commas should be inserted after the words "ripe" "sweet" and "crisp" because these adjectives are in a series.

5. (3), A comma should be inserted after "possible" because "If possible" is an introductory phrase. Introductory phrases can also be dependent clauses.

LESSON 6, pp. 106–107

1. (4), Quotation marks should be inserted around "When you say no, mean it" because it is direct speech from Mrs. Morgan.

2. (2), A comma should be inserted after "says" because "Dr. Harvey Jones says" is an introductory phrase. Also, quotation marks should be inserted around "Teaching our children to eat well is the most important thing we can do for them" because it is direct speech from Dr. Jones.

3. (3), A colon should be inserted at the end of sentence 5 because the sentence is introducing a list and examples.

4. (1), Sentence 8 is asking a question; therefore the period at the end of the question should be replaced with a question mark.

UNIT REVIEW, pp. 108–113

1. (1), The noun "Nutrition Label" is not a proper noun, therefore it does not need to be capitalized.

2. (5), Answer option 5 is correct because the first letter of the first word is capitalized, there is a comma after the introductory word, and the sentence ends with the correct punctuation.

3. (2), The semicolon in sentence 4 should be replaced with a colon because the clause that follows is an example.

4. (3), The correct contraction of the underlined portion is *you'll* because it is short for the phrase *you will*.

5. (2), The word "good" in sentence 11 does not have the correct punctuation marks. Quotation marks should appear before and after the word; therefore the apostrophe after "good" should be replaced with a quotation mark.

6. (4), The contraction "you're" is short for *you are* and you wouldn't say *increase you are intake*; therefore the correct word for sentence 7 is the possessive pronoun "your" to indicate possession of the intended subject's "intake."

7. (5), Sentence 2 does not contain any errors; therefore no correction is necessary.

8. (1), The misspelled word in sentence 6 is "valueble," which is spelled *valuable*.

9. (1), A comma should be inserted after "measure" because "As a preventative measure" is an introductory phrase. Introductory phrases can also be dependent clauses.

10. (3), The word "then" should be replaced with the word "than" because *then* indicates time and *than* indicates reference or comparison: *She was younger then; She is younger than me*.

11. (2), A colon should be inserted after "immediately" because examples follow.

12. (1), The possessive pronoun "its" should be replaced with the contraction "it's" because sentence 15 does not indicate possession.

13. (2), The word "Texarkana" should be capitalized because it is a proper noun.

14. (2), The period at the end of sentence 3 should be replaced with a colon because the following clause is a list of examples.

15. (1), The colons in sentence 4 should be replaced with semicolons because they are not each introducing an example, they are the example. Also, semicolons can be used instead of commas within a series when other internal punctuation is used.

16. (3), In the context of sentence 5, "advisor's" does not need to be in the possessive form because the sentence does not indicate possession; therefore "advisor's" should be replaced with the plural noun "advisors," which indicates more than one advisor.

17. (4), The homograph "too" means also. You wouldn't say *The also accounts*; therefore "too" should be replaced with "two," indicating an amount.

18. (5), This sentence does not contain any errors; therefore no correction is necessary.

Index

Note: Page numbers in **boldface** indicate definitions or main discussions. Page numbers in *italic* indicate a visual representation. Pages ranges indicate examples and practice.

A

Adjectives, **39**
    combining with hyphen, 106
    misplaced, 54–55
    proper, **95**, 96–97
Adverbs, **39**
    misplaced, 54–55
Analogies, **8**
Analysis, **21**
Anecdote, **4**
Antecedent, **67**, **72**, 72–73
Apostrophe, 98–99

B

Body of essay, 1, **6**, 6–7, 8–9, 12–15
    paragraphs of, 22–23, 28–29, 30–31
    supporting details, 26–27

C

Capitalization, **96**, 96–97
    of days of the week, 96
    of first word in quotations, 96
    of first word of sentences, 96
    of holidays, 96
    of I, 96
    of months, 96–97
    of proper adjectives, 96–97
    of proper nouns, 68, 96–97
    of titles, 96
Checklists
    for body paragraphs, 14
    for conclusion, 14
    for essay, 12
    for introduction, 14
    for review, 14
Clauses, **21**
    combining, 50–51
    in comma splices, 52
    in complex sentences, 48–49
    in compound sentences, 46–47
    as sentence fragments, 42–43
Coherence, **30**, 30–31
Collective nouns, **74**, 74–75
Colons, **95**, 106

Combining sentences, **50**, 50–51

Commas, **21**, **104**, 104–105
    combining sentences with, 50–51, 52–53
    in complex sentences, 48–49, 104–105
    in compound sentences, 46–47, 104
    following introductory word/phrase, 104–105
    in series, 104–105
    setting off interrupting phrases, 104–105
    setting off quotations, 104
Comma splice, **52**
Commonly misspelled words, 102–103
Complete sentences, **40**, 40–41
Complex sentences, **48**, 48–49, 104–105
Compound sentences, **46**, 46–47, 104
Compound subject, **67**, **84**
Compound words, possessives of, 98
Conclusion, 1, **10**, 10–11, 12–15
Conjunctions
    combining sentences with, 50–51, 52–53
    conjunctive adverbs, **39**, 46–47
    coordinating, **39**, 46–47, 50–51, 52–53
    correcting comma splice with, 52
    correcting run-on sentence with, 52–53
    sentence fragments and, 42–43
    subject-verb agreement and, 84–85
    subordinating, **39**, 48–49
Conjunctive adverbs, **39**, 46–47
Contractions, **98**, 98–99, 100
    its/it's, 98, 100
    their/they're, 100
    your/you're, 98–99, 100
Coordinating conjunction, **39**
    combining sentences with, 50–51, 52–53
    in compound sentences, 46–47
    correcting comma splices with, 52
    correcting run-on sentences, 52–53
    subject-verb agreement and, 84–85
Co-possessives, 98

D

Dangling modifiers, **56**, 56–57
Dashes, **95**, 106
Dependent clauses, **39**
    in complex sentences, 48–49
    as sentence fragments, 42–43

E

-ed, 78–79, 80–81
Editing, viii
Elaboration, **8**, 8–9, 14–15
End marks, 40, 44–45, 106–107
Essay, vii
    body, 1, **6**, 6–7, 8–9, 12–15
    conclusion, 1, **10**, 10–11, 12–15
    elaboration, 8–9, 12–15
    hook, **4**, 4–5, 12–15
    introduction, 1, **4**, 4–5, 12–15

prompts, 3, 5, 7, 9, 11, 15
review and revise, **12**, 12–15
scoring of, 12, 14
supporting details, 1, **2**, 4–5, 6–7, 8–9, 12–15, 26–27
text division, **22**, 22–23
thesis statement, 1, **2**, 2–3, 4–5, 12–15
time management of, 12
topic sentence, 24–25
transition, 6–7, 10–11, 12–15, 28–29
unity and coherence of, 30–31
See also Organization; Paragraphs; Sentence structure
Exclamation point, 40–41, 106–107

F

Facts, **21**
Feminine pronouns, 70–71
First-person narrative, **67**
Fragments, 42–43
Frontmatter
    About the GED Tests, iv–v
        subject-area breakdown, iv
    About *GED Xcelerator*, vi
    About *GED Xcelerator Writing*, vii–ix
    Copyright/Acknowledgements, ii
    Study Skills, xi
    Table of Contents, iii
    Test-Taking Tips, x
    Title Page, i
Future perfect tense, **80**, 80–81
Future tense, 76–77

G

GED Journeys
    Anderson, Walter, 94
    Burroughs, Augusten, 38
    Cosby, Bill, BLIND
    Jennings, Peter, 20
    LL Cool J, 66
GED Tests
    construction of, iv
    number of people taking/year, vi
    number of people who passed in 2007, vi
    preparation for, xi
    subjects tested/number of questions per subject, iv
    time limits for, iv
Gender
    pronoun agreement, 72–73
    of pronouns, 72–73
Glossary of terms, 1, 21, 39, 67, 95
Grammar, viii
    for essay writing, 12
    exceptions to rules, ix
Graphic organizers, for essay writing, *1, 2, 4, 6, 8, 10, 12*

INDEX